BABY'S NAMES
~& STAR SIGNS~

BABY'S NAMES
~& STAR SIGNS~

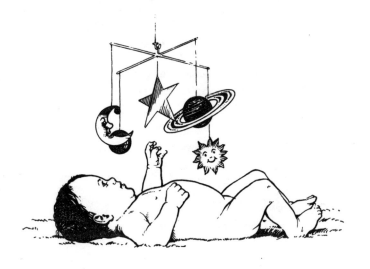

Sylvana Nown

WARD LOCK LIMITED · LONDON

© Ward Lock 1989
© Illustrations Ward Lock 1989

First published in Great Britain in 1989
by Ward Lock Limited, 8 Clifford Street
London W1X 1RB, an Egmont Company

Illustrations by Tony Randell

Text filmset in Sabon roman
by MS Filmsetting Limited, Frome, Somerset
Printed and bound in Great Britain by
William Collins and Sons & Co Ltd

British Library Cataloguing in Publication Data

Nown, Sylvana
     Baby's names and star signs—(Family matters)
     1. Names
     I. Title   II. Series
     929.9'7

ISBN 0-7063-6801-0

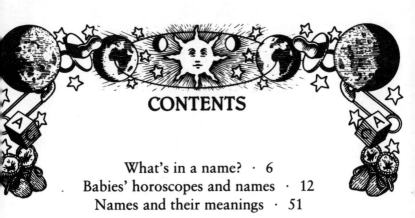

CONTENTS

WHAT'S IN A NAME?

Expecting a baby is an exciting milestone, and a time for wondering. What will he or she become? Will fate treat him or her kindly, bestowing abundant health and wealth? Astrology can hold a key to many of the answers but, perhaps more importantly to prospective parents, the twelve signs of the Zodiac can give an uncanny indication of character.

Will your baby blissfully sleep the clock round, or be a demanding little handful? His or her character may be shaped to a greater extent by the sun sign under which he or she is born. Cancer kids, for example, may be clinging, but kind and caring, while Aries babies might well be impatient bundles of energy. A tiny Virgo may be orderly to the point of picking up crumbs as she learns to crawl. Scorpios, on the other hand, could turn out to be self-willed and unwilling to share their toys.

Some people find that the sound of a name, too, can have a subtle effect on a child. To older ears some of them, in a lighthearted way, convey an idea of character. Hugh tends to sound rather solid and serious, while Mollie somehow hints at a loveable, carefree nature. An important point when you consider that Archie Leach was unheard of until he changed his name to Cary Grant. And Maurice Micklewhite was a struggling Smithfield porter until he became Michael Caine.

A combined study by San Diego and Georgia Universities revealed that teachers consistently gave lower marks to Elmers and Huberts than they did to Michaels and Davids. Girls with 'sexy' or popular names – such as Susan, Cheryl, Dawn or Heather – found it easier to progress in modelling than a business career.

In one way or another, we are all influenced by names more than we think, and parents should give careful consideration to what they intend to call their children. The Queen took a month on average to choose the names of each of her children. The Duke and Duchess of York took slightly longer before settling on Beatrice – Bringer of Joy – for their first child.

Before you make your final choice, always consider how the name matches your family name – there is no way of knowing what career your child might choose. Among those who omitted this basic point were the parents of A. Moron, the Commissioner of Education for the Virgin Islands; T. Hee, a New York waiter; Major Minor of the US Army and Cardinal Sin of the Diocese of Manila.

Not only is the sound of the name important and the way in which it combines with your surname, but there is the astrological consideration, too. To ensure that a chosen name has complete harmony it is worth looking at how it might be linked to the sign under which your baby is born.

There are several ways of doing this – the most obvious is by the use of a name directly connected to the time of year of baby's birthday. April or Avril, May and June, for instance, are often used for girls born in those particular months.

Lewis, or the female Louisa, and Lionel have leonine connections associated with children born under Leo.

Other 'calendar' names include Christmas, Noel or Nowell, for babies born on 25 December, and Stephen, which has been long associated with 26 December (the feast day of St Stephen). Easter is another pleasant name, but one which has never quite grown in popularity.

Dominic, meaning Sunday, and Tuesday – as in actress Tuesday Weld – have become the most popular names to commemorate the day on which baby came into the world.

For broader time periods there is Gavin, associated with the month of May; Verna, the girl's name from the

Latin for Spring; and Chloe, which means summertime. Dipping into the list of name origins at the back of this book may provide further inspiration for calendar names.

Settling on the name which sounds right for your child is an enjoyable business which is best not hurried. After all, it's a decision to last a lifetime. Take a leaf from the *Book of Proverbs:* 'A good name,' it advises, 'is rather to be chosen than great riches'.

Another astrological method is to consider a name linked to baby's Element. The Signs of the Zodiac are traditionally grouped under the four basic symbols of Earth, Air, Fire and Water in the following way:

EARTH	AIR	FIRE	WATER
Taurus	Gemini	Aries	Cancer
Virgo	Libra	Leo	Scorpio
Capricorn	Aquarius	Sagittarius	Pisces

The origins of most children's names derive from Greek, Latin, Hebrew or Celtic words which refer to aspects of nature or the universe. Lyn, for example, comes from the Anglo-Saxon for cascade, or waterfall – a Water element which may appeal to parents of babies born under Cancer, Scorpio or Pisces. In a similar vein, Leigh, or Lee, from the Anglo-Saxon for meadow, is linked to the Earth element and may suit Taurus, Virgo or Capricorn children. Because our ancestors were rural people, tied closely to the land, there is a preponderance of Earth names – George means Farmer; Hortense, Gardener; Stanley, Stoney Field and so on. Water names are also plentiful, with Air and Fire in the minority, but the choice is nevertheless generous and interesting.

In addition to being grouped under the Elements, each sign has a ruling Planet which influences baby's personality. Certain attributes or characteristics are associated with each ruling planet and these may express themselves from an early age.

Birth signs are governed in the following way:

ARIES by MARS
TAURUS by VENUS
GEMINI by MERCURY
CANCER by the MOON
LEO by the SUN
VIRGO by MERCURY
LIBRA by VENUS
SCORPIO by PLUTO and MARS
SAGITTARIUS by JUPITER
CAPRICORN by SATURN
AQUARIUS by URANUS
PISCES by NEPTUNE

The origins of certain names can be related to the influence of each ruling planet. An obvious example is Angela, from the Greek for Messenger. Mercury, the messenger of the gods, represents wit and intelligence, and an ability to communicate – an apt name for actress Angela Lansbury, star of the detective series *Murder She Wrote*. Meredith (Guardian of the Sea) is linked to the planet Neptune, which influences Pisceans, or Robert (Brightness) to the Sun, ruling planet of Leo.

It can be fun to link a name with the characteristics of the ruling planet of the sign under which your baby is born. If you like the sound of it, then the choice may turn out to be most appropriate.

Cecilia, or Cecily – the feminine form of Cecil – is another typical example. St Cecilia is the patron saint of music, and music, the arts – indeed anything connected to harmony and beauty – are governed by the planet Venus. Perhaps a perfect name for someone born under Taurus.

Checklists of the various starsign links can be found in the horoscope section of this book. In the meantime, here is a brief rundown of the characteristics associated with each ruling planet:

MARS: assertiveness, energy, action and drive.

VENUS: an interest in the arts and music; a contented, loving nature.

MERCURY: an ability to communicate, sharp wit and intelligence.

MOON: emotional moods, sensitive, responds to sympathy.

SUN: playful, self-expressive; a sunny nature with a dislike of being ignored.

PLUTO: changeable, emotionally intense.

JUPITER: optimistic, outward-looking, enthusiastic.

SATURN: cautious, learns from experience, far-sighted.

URANUS: independent, inventive, spontaneous.

NEPTUNE: rich imagination, not too practical but given to inspiration.

If you wish to link your baby's name to his or her astrological sign, you may broaden your choice by looking beyond connections with the ruling planet.

The original meanings of many popular names also relate to the general characteristics of each sign. We all know that Arians, for example, are home-loving, or that Virgoans are neat and clean. Scorpios, we find, may be rather intense and Cancerians old-fashioned and romantic.

Often a particular name may sum up such character snapshots and turn out to be most suitable for a child. Freda, meaning Peaceful, sums up the quiet nature of Pisceans. Hard-working Capricorns, on the other hand, may suit an unusual name like the old German 'Meyrick', meaning 'ruler of work', or for those Aries types who are born leaders Richard, meaning leader, or Melvin (chief) might be appropriate. Hunting for an astrological name can be both entertaining and give a fascinating insight into the way your child might develop. Another variation contained in some of the horoscope lists which follow is that of names connected to birth-stones.

Each sun sign traditionally has its own gemstone, but occasionally they vary from authority to authority. For the purpose of consistency those mentioned in this book are from the list commissioned by the National Association of Jewellers in 1923, and used by gem specialists ever since.

Good hunting.

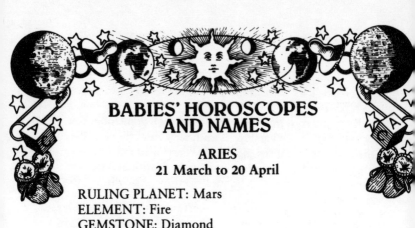

BABIES' HOROSCOPES AND NAMES

ARIES
21 March to 20 April

RULING PLANET: Mars
ELEMENT: Fire
GEMSTONE: Diamond

Aries parents may notice that their children bear a strange resemblance to their symbol of the ram. When their hair grows it often has a thick, fleecy quality. Many Aries babies have broad foreheads and, when they lose their chubby cheeks, elongated faces.

Rather like a ram battering at a farm gate, they can be impatient, determined babies who waste no time in letting you know who is in charge. Aries babies are known to yell lustily for attention and make very clear their preferences in food.

Despite their howls and tantrums, you will probably never get angry with them because angelic Aries faces can dissolve into the most engaging smiles when they get what they want.

If you should reach the conclusion that there is something of a little dictator in your Aries offspring, take heart – Aries children have a reputation for being born leaders. The way in which they tend to crash through their early years, dramatically demanding time and attention, demonstrates a forceful personality.

Beneath the bluster the security of a loving hand to hold is needed, however. Aries children appreciate a strong home life and the close protection of caring parents.

Just like the ram, they are headstrong and – a point to watch – quite accident prone. One consolation to emerge from all this is that their Mars-ruled constitution makes recovery from the usual run of childhood tumbles and illnesses little problem.

Aries children are adventurous and outgoing. So, as soon as they learn to walk – which may well be earlier than other children – you will have to be on full alert to avoid mishaps.

Little Ariens, and older ones, are essentially doers. Their active nature makes them easily bored with sitting around – and they will not be afraid to tell you so. They respond to parents who take time to play with them. One way to counterbalance that headstrong character, incidentally, is to appeal to their imagination by reading stories of fantasy and adventure. An Aries child will sit for hours engrossed in tales of elves, dragons and fairytale palaces.

Insensitivity is one of their bad points. Aries children tend to push their own needs to the fore and, in doing so, develop independence and self-expression quite early. Take care not to misinterpret this. They are generous in sharing their toys and extremely loving to those around them. Aries babies, if you are lucky to have one, are little handfuls with hearts of gold. Once they share your life you will never have a dull moment.

ARIES NAMES:

Archibald: Old German for Truly Bold

Aurelia: Latin for Golden Haired – traditionally an Arien feature

Chloe: The mythological shepherdess

Flora: Goddess of Springtime – the Aries season

Fraser: Old French meaning Curly Headed

Jason: Greek hero who recovered the Golden Fleece

Kimball: Old English for Royally Bold

Nora, Norah: Honour

Peter: Associations with the Arien trait of fearlessness

Piers: French form of Peter

Rachel: From the Hebrew for Ewe

FIRE NAMES:

Agatha: St Agatha was the protector against fire
Aileen: From the Greek for Light of Brightness
Edna: From the Celtic for Fire

MARS NAMES:

Donovan: Celtic for Dark Warrior
Duncan: Old Irish – Brown Warrior
Edith: Old English for Prosperous War
Gerald: The Power of the Spear in Old German
Harold: Powerful Warrior in Norse
Kelly: Irish meaning War
Marcia: Evolved from Mars, God of War
Mark: Mars, Roman God of War
Martin: Meaning of Mars

FAMOUS ARIENS:

Elton John	Vincent Van Gogh
Marlon Brando	Peter Ustinov
David Frost	Michael Heseltine
Bette Davis	Andrew Lloyd Webber
Alec Guinness	David Steel
Hans Christian Andersen	Spike Milligan
Charlie Chaplin	Ruth Madoc
Julie Christie	James Garner
Joan Crawford	Ali MacGraw

TAURUS
21 April to 20 May

RULING PLANET: Venus
ELEMENT: Earth
GEMSTONE: Emerald

Bringing up a Taurus baby is rather like leading a young bull to a field. Taurus babies are calm, obedient and well-behaved – until pushed. Once force is used, nothing will make them give way, from pulling on their pyjamas, to eating up their greens or saying sorry.

Taurus children like to be told why they have to do something – 'Because I say so' is not quite good enough. If your explanation seems reasonable, or logical, they will usually comply without a murmur. In other words, Taureans need a certain amount of handling. Once you understand their character they are adorable children who love nothing more than to cuddle or be cuddled.

Like their element Earth, they are practical, down-to-basics little people and you will have no trouble encouraging them to do useful jobs around the house.

In keeping with their bull sign they are quiet, sociable and express their herd instinct in an appreciation of home life and strong family relationships. Most of the time, Taureans will be well-mannered and obedient – rarely the rebel who wanders off to climb into cupboards or breaks things around the house.

The other side of their nature comes into play only when they are pushed into doing something against their will – then you see the classic Taurean stubborness surface. A May baby will submit to nappy changes without fuss, if it suits. But if woken, or if play at nappy time is interrupted, a Taurean baby will resist with every ounce of strength.

Being the parent of a Taurus baby requires a certain degree of psychology but, once a request makes sense, cooperation will be affectionate in a way which will make you glow with pride. Any attempt at coercion and heels will be dug in.

These displays of wilful determination, however, are the exception rather than the rule. Taurus children do not generally have wild swings of mood. Most of the time they are quiet, contented and influenced by harmonious things around them.

Taureans react in a particularly positive way to colour. Pastel shades bring out the placid side of their nature. They respond in a similar way to the arts and tend to be quick learners with a paintbrush or musical instrument. Anything connected with peace and harmony appeals. Harsh reds and oranges, shrill voices or loud, discordant music make them withdraw.

On the health point, it is worth noting that Taureans have a weakness around the neck, and may be prone to traditional childhood illnesses associated with that area – mumps, ear-ache, tonsillitis and sore throats.

Curiously, when they grow older, men often have strong, stocky necks and women the graceful, swanlike necks of models.

TAUREAN NAMES:
Cecilia, Cecily: St Cecilia is the Patron Saint of Music, a common Taurean talent

Drew: From the Old French for Sturdy

Emily: Industrious – Taureans are the hard workers of the Zodiac

Gavin: Hawk of May, the Taurean month

Penelope, Penny: Penelope waited ten years for her husband Odysseus – patience is a Taurean trait

EARTH NAMES:
Aaron: High mountain

Adam: Thought to be Red Earth, or Dust

Ashley: Field of Ash in Anglo Saxon

Blodwen: Welsh for White Flower

Carmel: From the Hebrew for Vineyard

Clifford: Old English for Dweller on a Slope
Craig: Crag, rugged rock
Daisy: Flower name
Dale: Dweller in a valley
Elton: Anglo Saxon for Old Settlement
Erica: Latin for Heather
Ester, Hester: Persian for Myrtle
Fabian, Fabia: The grower
George: From the Greek for Farmer
Glen, Glyn: Welsh for Valley
Hazel: After the tree
Heather: After the plant
Holly: After the plant
Iris: Flower name
Ivy: After the plant
Jasmine: After the plant
Laura: After the bay tree Laurel
Laurence: Associated with Laurel
Lee, Leigh: Old English for Meadow
Lily, Lillian: Flower name
Linette: From the Latin for Flax
Marigold: Flower name
Olive, Olivia, Oliver: After the olive tree
Peter: The Rock
Phyllis: Greek for Green Leaf
Piers: French for Peter, the rock
Primrose: Flower name
Quentin: Celtic for Hound of the Meadow
Rhoda, Rosalie, Rosalind, Rosamund, Rose: Associated with roses
Rosemary: Flower name
Ross: Gaelic meaning Of The Peninsular
Russell: The fox
Shelley: A wood
Shirley: Shire meadow
Silvia, Sylvia: Of the wood
Stanley: Stone Field in Anglo Saxon

Susan: From the Hebrew for Lily
Teresa: From the Greek for Reaper
Viola, Violet: Flower name
Wilbur: Wild farmer
Yasmine: Flower name

VENUS NAMES:
Ada: Old German for Happy
Amanda: From the Latin verb to Love
Annabel, Annabella: Grace and beauty
Catherine: From the Greek for Purity
Charity: Love in early Latin and Greek
Darrell, Daryl: Old English for Darling, Beloved
Melody, Melodie: Associated with harmony
Ruth: Vision of beauty
Sheree, Sherri, Sherry: Dear one
Una: Truth

FAMOUS TAUREANS:

Barbra Streisand	John Mortimer
William Shakespeare	Glen Campbell
Yehudi Menuhin	Dickie Davies
Audrey Hepburn	Victoria Wood
Margot Fonteyn	Toyah Wilcox
Her Majesty the Queen	Johannes Brahms
Fred Astaire	Karl Marx

GEMINI
21 May to 20 June

RULING PLANET: Mercury
ELEMENT: Air
GEMSTONE: Pearl or Agate

Your challenge will start when your Gemini baby begins to talk. The Geminian ruling planet of Mercury provides a talent for communication and, as soon as your baby can string a sentence together, wait for the Whys, Wheres and Hows.

Gemini babies can be tiring because they appear to have limitless reserves of energy. Even in later life Gemini adults are often fidgety and have quick, nervous movements. In children, much of this is creative energy looking for expressive outlets.

Gemini children are inquisitive chatterboxes but, unlike some signs of the Zodiac, do not mind in the least if they are passed around the family for everyone to hold. Movement and activity simply feeds their natural curiosity about people.

Gemini is, of course, the sign of twins and there is a curious old wives' tale, which statistics have done nothing to diminish, that June is a favourite month for giving birth to them. Parents of Gemini twins will certainly have their hands full. One little Gemini is a full-time task for any mother.

With Air as the Gemini element, all babies born under this sign like plenty of space to move around in and to make the most of it. Few Gemini babies will sit placidly in a playpen, like Taureans, once they learn to crawl. Their natural curiosity and quick minds take them all over the house, examining anything which may look interesting. So, take extra care with matches, plugs, open fires and safety in general. Gemini kids love television, radio and telephones and will try to play with them as toddlers.

You will have to live in the fast lane to keep up with Gemini children but, instead of trying to change their essential nature, insist on periods of rest. Regular bedtimes provide a much-needed respite from that reservoir of energy.

Their ruling sign Mercury makes them quick, enthusiastic learners, anxious to soak up knowledge and try out new things. Teachers love them and, if you are prepared to devote the time, your Gemini baby's sharp understanding will never cease to entertain and amaze you.

Because of their aptitude for communication, some of the best actors and salesmen are Geminis. In childhood the talent expresses itself in various ways – a keen sense of humour, marvellous mimicry and a love of losing themselves in fantasy, from daydreams to storybooks and pantomimes. On the negative side, they may turn around their skills when in trouble and tell the most convincing fibs.

Because Geminis flit from one interest to another they may lack concentration. With care it is possible to encourage patience and consistency without curbing their natural desire to enquire about everything.

GEMINI NAMES:

Denis, Dennis, Denys: After the God of Revelry, indicating Geminis' stimulating, vivacious nature
Jacob: The twin of Esau
June: The month of Gemini
Pearl: A Gemini gemstone
Vivian: From the Latin for lively

AIR NAMES:

Eve, Eva: From the Irish for Sunlight
Fay, Faye: Fairy, spirit of the air
Keith: Gaelic for Wind
Lucille, Lucy: Light
Melissa: Greek meaning a Bee

MERCURY NAMES:

Angela: From the Greek for Messenger

Belinda: Associated with Snake, part of Mercury's symbol

Camilla, Camille: Fleet of foot

Linda: Old German for Serpent, associated with Mercury's symbol

FAMOUS GEMINIS:

Bob Dylan	Ian Fleming
Rudolph Valentino	Duke of Edinburgh
Cole Porter	Arthur Conan Doyle
Marilyn Monroe	Nigel Davenport
John F. Kennedy	Joan Collins
Bob Hope	Cilla Black
Judy Garland	James Bolam
Thomas Hardy	Bob Monkhouse

CANCER
21 June to 20 July

RULING PLANET: The Moon
ELEMENT: Water
GEMSTONE: Ruby

No baby is perfect, but if your ideal child is warm, caring, full of love and with a wonderful imagination, then you may be close to your dream with a Cancerian. There is one small problem – children born under the sign of the crab are sensitive souls. At the slightest indication of anything hurtful they may withdraw into their shell.

Cancerian babies, like adults, have something of a reputation for fine skin, often pale and milky, with round faces like their ruling planet, the Moon.

Because they can be easily hurt or misunderstood, Cancer children tend to remember all of life's little troughs and peaks. They develop extremely long memories which, in later life, display themselves in a love of nostalgia. Like the crab, which carries its house on its back, the emotional atmosphere at home is crucial to a Cancer child.

He may be shy and occasionally moody. He may not be as demonstrative as other signs, but he needs as much, if not more, affection. Here a fine balance must be found between love and over-protection because Cancerians, in keeping with the crab, can be clinging individuals.

Tears are often associated with the Moon and there may be rivers of them if he does not get his own way. The motive is usually for attention and affection.

Cancer children tend to pick their friends carefully. They are not boisterous, trailing around masses of playmates, but quite content in their own company playing games of imagination for hours. This is part of the Cancerian children's character and should not be misinterpreted as loneliness.

Because of their withdrawn ways, little Cancerians positively blossom with praise. They like to be reassured that they are lovely, clever, good or bright. Their response, however, makes it easy to go too far and pamper them.

When the first day of playschool comes around, their powerful dependence on their parents may make it difficult to place them on their own two feet. But, with care and understanding, they will develop into compassionate, home-loving children, less likely to take off into the wide blue yonder than some other star signs. This applies especially to Cancerians born in July.

The fine side of their character will often show in a love of animals – Cancerians adore pets – or if a member of the family falls ill. The moody side of little Cancerians is soon pushed aside by the kind-hearted nurse in them.

With the right family environment they will always return wherever they wander – and never fail to amuse you. That elephant memory and love of nostalgia often prompts them to ask what happened to the doll or favourite toy car you may have thrown out years earlier.

CANCER NAMES:
Alastair: Unforgetting one – an apt reminder of the long Cancerian memory
Clemence, Clement: Latin for Mildness, Merciful
Delia: Reserved and Faithful in Greek
Freda: Peaceful
Giles: A servant – Cancer is associated with service and domesticity
June: A Cancerian month
Leanna, Leanne: Clinging vine – Cancerians often have a clinging nature
Ruby: The Cancer gemstone

WATER NAMES:
Brook(e): Dweller at a watercourse
Doris, Dorise: Sea Nymph

Douglas: A Celtic river
Dylan: Legendary sea god
Irving: Sea Friend in Old English
Kelvin: Gaelic for Narrow Stream
Lyn: Waterfall
Mary: Star of the sea
Meredith: Guardian from the sea
Mervyn, Marvin: Sea hill
Morgan: Seabright
Muriel: Sea
Murray: Sea, Sea Warrior in Celtic
Norman: God of the Sea in Old German
Roland: Old Welsh for the Torrent
Rosemary: Dew of the sea
Winifred: Welsh for White Stream

MOON NAMES:

Cynthia: From the Greek for Moon
Myra: Latin for She Who Weeps – tears have long been associated with the Moon
Phoebe: Greek Moon goddess
Selina: Also from the Greek for Moon

FAMOUS CANCERIANS:

Princess Diana	Barbara Stanwyck
Ringo Starr	George Orwell
Julius Caesar	Willie Whitelaw
Ernest Hemingway	Cyril Smith
Helen Keller	Natalie Wood
Gina Lollobrigida	Nelson Mandela
Duke of Windsor	David Owen

LEO
21 July to 21 August

RULING PLANET: The Sun
ELEMENT: Fire
GEMSTONE: Peridot or Sardonyx

Bringing up an August child may at times feel like putting your head in a lion's mouth. They can be bossy with other children and roar loudly for your attention, but there is the compensation of a sunny, attentive nature guaranteed to melt your heart.

A certain amount of discipline is required in raising a Leo – too little and you may find yourself at your baby's beck and call, too much and your little lion will feel unloved.

There are two sides to the Leo personality which emerge early in childhood. At their best they have bags of confidence and enthusiasm and can be generous and loving. The flipside of the Leo coin is domineering, cheekily arrogant and selfish. The trick lies in coaxing out the good qualities without entirely suppressing their natural high spirits.

Just like the lion, which has boundless energy followed by periods of lethargy, Leos have their lazy days, when toys are not put away and books are left scattered on the floor. They are quite happy to sit around and watch you pick them up, unless you give a gentle nudge in the right direction.

The little Leo likes to be leader of the pack and, in the case of girls, there may even be a brief tomboy period. Leos are often hurt when they learn that they cannot be in charge all the time but they come to terms with it.

Being a leader is another way of becoming the centre of attention. Leos love the limelight and have no difficulty in coping with compliments. Criticism, on the other hand, is often badly received, especially when it may involve loss of face in front of others.

The Leo personality may express itself in a child who loves bossing others around, or in the quieter, loving type who likes to be at the centre of things. Either way, Leos are sure to have a sunny nature, oodles of charm from babyhood, and a winning smile to melt the hardest heart.

Physically, they may grow to be very leonine, with luxuriant hair and a proud, confident walk. Leo kids will always wear you out before they become exhausted. They have strong constitutions, but periods of rest and calm are of great importance to growing cubs.

LEO NAMES:
Albert: Noble splendour
Amos: A name associated with strength
Basil: From the Greek meaning Kingly
Conal: Celtic for High-Mighty
Leo, Leon: From the Greek and Latin meaning Lion
Leonard: Lion-hearted
Lionel: Young lion
Louis: Praise and fame – much-loved by Leos
Mark: A winged lion was the symbol of St Mark
Miranda: To be admired – a topic close to Leos' hearts
Richard: The Lionheart
Sebastian: Sacred majesty
Vincent: Conquering in Latin

FIRE NAMES:
Agatha: St Agatha, protector against fire
Aileen: From the Greek for Light or Brightness
Edna: From the Celtic for Fire

SUN NAMES:
Arnold: Old German for Power
Brian: From the Celtic for Strength
Reginald: Power, Force in Old English
Robert, Roberta: Old German for Bright
Thomas: From the Phoenician for Sun God

FAMOUS LEOS:

The Queen Mother
Princess Margaret
Alan Whicker
Napoleon Bonaparte
Fidel Castro
Jackie Kennedy
George Bernard Shaw
Mae West
Cat Stevens
Jimmy Hill

Graham Gooch
Mick Jagger
Daley Thompson
Kate Bush
Julia Foster
Terry Wogan
Nigel Mansell
Madonna
Robert de Niro

VIRGO
22 August to 22 September

RULING PLANET: Mercury
ELEMENT: Earth
GEMSTONE: Sapphire

Virgoans are the Zodiac's perfectionists. Nothing is too small to be overlooked by their tidy minds. Don't be too surprised if your tiny Virgo, learning to crawl, pauses to pick up pieces of fluff from the carpet. Tidyness is a Virgo trait.

Food is always a problem with Virgoans. They are extremely fussy about what they eat. The things they do like invariably have to be cooked in a certain way – no lumps in the mashed potatoes or burnt edges on the toast. It is small wonder that the mums of some Virgos consider themselves lucky to find something their children like. Many Virgos are vegetarians, so don't be too surprised if you find yourself cooking one menu for the family and a different meal for your September offspring.

Virgoans have tidy minds as well as tidy habits. They like to question the facts they quickly absorb to ensure that there are no loose ends in their understanding of a topic. They are keen to help and accept orders without argument. While they seldom question your authority, their lively Mercury-inspired minds constantly seek answers to everything else.

Virgo sits in the sixth house of the Zodiac, which predominantly represents work, of one kind of another. Little Virgoans, especially girls, love to help with jobs around the house. Even as toddlers they are happy to follow mum with a duster or lend a hand at rolling out pastry. They are seldom untidy and, while it is impossible to expect children to be neat all the time, their bedroom will generally have everything in its place.

Virgoans are loving and caring and happy to share

things – but every book or toy lent to a friend is carefully filed in that orderly memory. Because they like everything to be done correctly they can become over critical. One way to temper this is to make them aware that they must be prepared to be criticized themselves if they have the same attitude to others. If the trait goes too far you may have a constant complainer on your hands.

One emotional point about Virgoans which sets them apart from other signs is that they seldom demonstrate their love openly. This should not be misunderstood as a lack of affection. On the contrary, they value the security of family life highly and expect plenty of hugs themselves.

Their sensitivity sometimes makes them slightly withdrawn and shy in company. Virgoans are amusing children with their highly-developed sense of duty and responsibility and their rather serious view of life. Despite their fastidiousness they have a remarkable ability to fit into any change of scene or last minute plans, which makes them a delight to take anywhere.

VIRGO NAMES:

Alma: Latin for Fair, and Celtic for All Good, a Maiden

Amelia: Old German for Worker – Virgo, in the sixth House, represents Service, Work and Wealth

Amos: Bearer of burdens – Virgos will take on others' problems

Angela: Angel – for Virgoans' peaceful, heavenly qualities

Cassandra: Greek for Helper of Men

Lance: From the Latin meaning Servant

Martha: Aramaic meaning Lady

Ruth: Hebrew for Vision of Beauty

Simone: Obedient

Unity: Perfection – Virgoans are the ultimate perfectionists

Virginia: Virgin

EARTH NAMES:

Aaron: High mountain
Adam: Thought to originate from Red Earth, or Dust
Ashley: Field of Ash in Anglo Saxon
Blodwen: From the Welsh for White Flower
Carmel: Old Hebrew for Vineyard
Clifford: Dweller on a Slope in Old English
Craig: Crag, rugged rock
Daisy: Flower name
Dale: Dweller in a valley
Elton: Old Settlement in Anglo Saxon
Erica: Latin for Heather
Ester, Hester: Originally Persian for Myrtle
Fabian, Fabia: The grower
Fleur: French for Flower
George: From the Greek for Farmer
Glen, Glyn: Welsh for Valley
Hazel: After the tree
Heather: After the plant
Holly: After the plant
Iris: Flower name
Ivy: After the plant
Jasmine: After the plant
Laura: After the bay tree Laurel
Laurence: Associated with Laurel
Lee, Leigh: Old English for Meadow
Lily, Lilian: Flower name
Linette: From the Latin for Flax
Marigold: Flower Name
Olive, Olivia, Olivia: After the olive tree
Peter: The Rock
Phyllis: Greek for Green Leaf
Piers: French for Peter, the rock
Ross: From the Gaelic, meaning Of The Peninsular
Russell: The fox
Shelley: A wood
Silvia, Sylvia: Of the wood

Stanley: Stone Field in Anglo Saxon
Susan: From the Hebrew for Lily
Teresa: The Reaper in early Greek
Viola, Violet: Flower name
Wilbur: Wild farmer
Yasmine: Flower name

MERCURY NAMES:

Angela: Originally Greek for Messenger
Belinda: Associated with snake, part of Mercury's symbol
Camilla, Camille: Fleet of foot
Linda: Old German for Serpent, associated with Mercury's symbol

FAMOUS VIRGOANS:

Queen Elizabeth I
Sophia Loren
Peter Sellers
Lauren Bacall
Ingrid Bergman
Dr Rob Buckman
Jean-Michel Jarre
Leonard Bernstein
Frederick Forsyth
Elliott Gould

Michael Jackson
Lenny Henry
James Coburn
Judy Geeson
Kenneth Lo
Angus Ogilvy
Jeremy Irons
Jimmy Young
Pauline Collins

LIBRA
23 September to 22 October

RULING PLANET: Venus
ELEMENT: Air
GEMSTONE: Opal

Librans have the sign of the scales, a symbol which sums up their personality from an early age. Those born under the sign of Libra are apt to weigh the pros and cons with great deliberation. They can often be indecisive, and pressure to solve too many problems, or make immediate choices, may put them under strain. This is something which can be overcome with an understanding of the Libran's up and down nature.

One way in which the scales influence October children is that they spend time assessing things to the point of becoming slowcoaches – what games to play, which clothes to wear, what flavour to choose from a milkshake menu. All the chiding in the world will not hurry them. But because they may be the last of the family to climb into the car, or take longer selecting coloured pencils, does not mean that they are lazy or intellectually slow. Librans simply prefer to live at their own pace rather than someone else's.

Underlying this influence on their character is an extremely logical mind. The Libran prefers to know all sides of an issue before reaching a conclusion. He is more interested in the background to a story than the headlines. Gossip, or one-sided news, tends to irritate him. Your young Libran will put forward lively arguments in favour of the underdog. At school, October children enjoy class discussions and debates. Even as toddlers they can be persuasive when putting a point across.

All this, of course, is helped enormously by Librans' ruling planet Venus, which imbues them with winning charm. They have a smile which makes people lower the defences.

Parents of Libran children may look back and thankfully recall how less accident-prone than others their offspring were. This is largely due to Librans' inbuilt caution and reluctance to be led into risk.

Eventually, these emotional scales will become perfectly balanced if the home environment is harmonious. They are easily thrown out of equilibrium by discord of any kind – from family rows to unpleasant music.

Perhaps because of this, little Librans respond in a positive way to colours – they prefer peaceful and harmonious shades. Show them a selection of colour schemes and ask which they like – their choice will be typically ruled by the Venus love of beauty and peace.

LIBRA NAMES:
Alexander, Alexandra: Protector of men
Daniel: From the Hebrew meaning a Judge
Iona: Violet coloured – a Libran shade
Melody, Melodie: Associated with harmony, balance
Veronica: Latin meaning a True Image

AIR NAMES:
Eve, Eva: From the Irish for Sunlight
Fay, Faye: Fairy, spirit of the air
Keith: Gaelic for the Wind
Lucille, Lucy: Light
Melissa: From the Greek meaning Bee

VENUS NAMES:
Ada: Old German for Happy
Amanda: From the Latin verb to Love
Annabel, Annabella: Grace and beauty
Catherine: From the Greek for Purity
Charity: Love in early Greek and Latin
Darrell, Daryl: Old English for Darling, Beloved
Ruth: Vision of beauty
Sheree, Sherri, Sherry: Dear one
Una: Truth

FAMOUS LIBRANS:

Julie Andrews
T. S. Eliot
John Lennon
Brigitte Bardot
Michelle Dotrice
Lech Walesa
Ian Ogilvy
Catherine Deneuve
Evel Knievel

Rita Hayworth
Chris de Burgh
Katherine Mansfield
Rick Parfitt
Daniel Massey
Donald Sinden
Gerry Adams
Anneka Rice

SCORPIO
23 October to 22 November

RULING PLANET: Pluto/Mars
ELEMENT: Water
GEMSTONE: Topaz

The first point to remember about Scorpio babies is that they have enormous reserves of emotional energy and are often strong physically.

Enchanting, entertaining Scorpio children have mysterious depths and powerful personalities, even as toddlers. Most become adept at concealing their thoughts, but little can hide Scorpio's most noticeable characteristic – an unswerving, penetrating gaze. There will be times when you wonder what is going on inside your baby's tiny head as those magnetic eyes look up at you. On other occasions they might fix you in a battle of wills.

Because of their inner strength, Scorpios tend to be determined individuals, so a well thought-out strategy of discipline is important. They will not be browbeaten into doing what you want but, when love and under-standing are shown, they are happy to comply.

Never forget, however, that beneath that normally placid surface, deep emotional currents swirl. With the wrong handling, Scorpios can become full of their own self-importance, jealous and unforgiving. If someone upsets your little Scorpio at playschool, he will bear it stoically. Underneath, the incident will not be forgotten until he can take revenge. This, of course, is a trait which should not be encouraged. With Scorpios success can be achieved only in positive ways with a little logic and a lot of patience.

November children, it is said, traditionally make good journalists. The truth of the adage can be seen from an early age. They have bright, sharp minds and an intense curiosity about everything around them.

One way in which to temper the negative side of the Scorpio nature is to channel mental and emotional energies into creative interests – anything connected with mysteries, puzzles or problems which require clever solving, for example, will happily occupy and stimulate young Scorpios who can spend hours entertaining themselves in this way.

Bringing up a Scorpio child is certainly a challenge. Life can be exhausting and occasionally a war of wills, but you will have the satisfaction of knowing that your child is like no other. A clever little individual who, in later life, will go after what he or she wants and invariably get it.

SCORPIO NAMES:
Alastair: Unforgetting one – an apt Scorpio name
Beryl: Believed by some to be the November gemstone
Conor: Indicates ambition, idealism

WATER NAMES:
Amaryllis: Sparkling stream in early Greek
Brook(e): Dweller at a watercourse
Doris, Dorise: Sea nymph
Douglas: A Celtic river
Dylan: Legendary sea god
Irving: Sea Friend in Old English
Kelvin: Gaelic for Narrow Stream
Lyn: Waterfall
Mary: Star of the sea
Meredith: Guardian from the sea
Mervyn, Marvin: Sea hill
Morgan: Seabright
Muriel: Sea
Murray: Sea, Sea Warrior in Celtic
Norman: God of the Sea in Old German
Roland: Old Welsh for Torrent
Rosemary: Dew of the sea
Winifred: Welsh for White Stream

PLUTO NAMES:

Anastasia: From the Greek for One Who Shall Rise Again

Daphne: In Greek mythology Daphne changed into a laurel bush – Pluto influences changeability

MARS NAMES:

Donovan: Celtic for Dark Warrior

Duncan: Old Irish – Brown Warrior

Edith: Old English for Prosperous War

Gerald: The Power of the Spear in Old German

Harold: Powerful Warrior in Norse

Kelly: Irish meaning War

Marcia: Evolved from Mars, God of War

Mark, Mars, Roman God of War

Martin: Meaning of wars

FAMOUS SCORPIOS:

Pablo Picasso
Martin Luther
Katharine Hepburn
Billy Graham
Prince Charles
Richard Burton
Telly Savalas
Goldie Hawn
Billie Jean King
Robert Vaughn

Robin Day
Simon le Bon
Evelyn Waugh
David Dimbleby
Burt Lancaster
Tatum O'Neal
Griff Rhys Jones
Alastair Cooke
John Cleese

SAGITTARIUS
23 November to 20 December

RULING PLANET: Jupiter
ELEMENT: Fire
GEMSTONE: Turquoise

One of the first things you may notice about Sagittarian babies are their beautiful smiles. Many astrologers liken little Sagittarians to clowns – a beaming smile with the hint of a tear lurking behind it.

What is perhaps more appropriate is the Sagittarian symbol itself – the archer, half man half horse, with a drawn bow. The centaur sums up perfectly the dual nature of December children. The human half of their sign denotes a love of company and a sociable nature. But somewhere there is a wild horse yearning for the open spaces.

Sagittarians love the freedom of the outdoors and it is no coincidence that the sign is connected with exploration. Without a sharp eye, your toddling offspring may take to wandering away to investigate the intriguing world outside. Sagittarians are not, however, as strong-headed as their sun sign stable-mates Scorpio, and a gentle word of warning will probably suffice.

The tears are sometimes easy to cope with – if you closely watch Sagittarian babies you will discover that they dislike being left alone. They will probably howl their heads off if left in the garden, but gurgle with contentment once wheeled into a roomful of people. Sagittarians are sociable creatures at heart, at their most relaxed in company.

When they are content, Sagittarians have a careful nature and a happy-go-lucky approach to life. Like their archer symbol, they shoot an arrow straight and true. Sagittarians have a high regard for honour, honesty and fair-play. They are extremely trustworthy themselves and expect the same from others.

Straight-dealing is something which they admire and respect. If someone is wrong and has the character to admit it – especially a parent – then they have won a Sagittarian friend and ally. Jupiter, their ruling planet, is traditionally the protector of justice so, in the eyes of a Sagittarian, everything has to be acceptable and above board.

Perhaps because of this in-built honesty and desire for truth, Sagittarian children are deeply inquisitive about every imaginable topic. As soon as baby begins to talk, life with a small Sagittarian becomes a daily inquisition of the most delightful kind. If you encourage their nimble minds you will find them amusing and endearing company.

SAGITTARIUS NAMES:
Alexander, Alexandra: Protector of men
Barry: From the Irish for Straight at the Mark
Hector: Gaelic meaning Horseman
Hunter: Old English name
Philip: Lover of horses
Ralf, Ralph: Wolf Counsel – Sagittarius is known as the Counsellor of the Zodiac
Raymond: Old English for Counsel Protection
Verity: Truth
Yvette, Yvonne: Old German for the Archer

JUPITER NAMES:
Edmund: Rich protection
Fergus: Man of Virtue in Celtic – Jupiter is the protector of virtue
Justin, Justine: Just – Jupiter is also the protector of justice

FIRE NAMES:
Agatha: St Agatha was the protector against fire
Aileen: From the Greek for Light or Brightness
Edna: From the Celtic for Fire

FAMOUS SAGITTARIANS:

Frank Sinatra	Ernie Wise
Lee Remick	Robert Dougall
Walt Disney	John Bunyan
Noel Coward	Keith Michell
Winston Churchill	Maria Callas
Beethoven	Jonathan King
Ian Botham	Alexander Solzhenitsyn
Billy Connolly	Keith Richards
Tina Turner	

CAPRICORN
21 December to 19 January

RULING PLANET: Saturn
ELEMENT: Earth
GEMSTONE: Garnet

One of the mysteries of having a January baby is that there are times when you wonder if you have a baby at all. Capricorns take life extremely seriously and, even as tiny children, usually seem older than they really are.

While you will be spared the temper tantrums and petulance of some sun signs, little Capricorns do not fill the house with laughter. They tend to weigh up situations, like wise old men, and answer questions very solemnly.

Once you have mastered the knack of living with these rather sombre and responsible children, you will discover that they seldom run with the pack, but prefer to have one or two close friends. Encourage them gently to join in communal activities, particularly in the open air. Quite often they opt for staying indoors on a sunny day rather than take part in the fun in the garden.

This aspect of their nature is really nothing to worry about. When it comes to school you will find that they take a responsible attitude to getting their books ready, sharing household tasks and doing their homework.

Capricorns are practical people. They will play games and take part in leisure activities if they have a sound purpose. Often they prefer to sketch, sew, cook or make something useful to playing tag or watching television.

They enjoy a home atmosphere as solid and dependable as themselves. In childhood, as in later life, they are industrious and accept hard work without hesitation. Beneath this there is strong ambition, a desire to succeed through effort. If taken too far it may develop into the unsociable face of Capricorn – the loner who rarely displays emotion.

There is a delicate path to tread in bringing up a January baby. Encouraging him to socialize will steer his ambition in the right direction. Capricorns have the sign of the goat – sure-footed, cautious and capable of scaling heights which would deter more faint-hearted members of the Zodiac family.

Capricorns' solid approach, practical nature and powerful drive help them to do well in business. But no matter how high they rise in the world they will always respect your advice. Capricorns look up to age and wisdom. As children they accept discipline; in later years they listen carefully to guidance. Your January baby will probably turn into the child of your dreams – even if life is taken seriously.

CAPRICORN NAMES:

Alwyn: Devoted friend

Ernest: Ernest, serious

Holly: The tree of the month of Capricorn

Nicholas, Nicola: A Christmas name for Capricorn's month

Noel: Christmas

Rebecca: Associated with faithfulness, a Capricorn trait

Robin: A traditional Christmas name

Stephen: St Stephen's Day falls in December

Tiffany: A name for Epiphany, which falls in Capricorn

William: Helmet of Will – for Capricorns' driving ambition

EARTH NAMES:

Aaron: High mountain

Adam: Red earth, dust

Ashley: Field of Ash in Anglo Saxon

Blodwen: Welsh for White Flower

Carmel: From the Hebrew for Vineyard

Clifford: Old English for Dweller on a Slope

Craig: Crag, rugged rock

Daisy: Flower name

Dale: Dweller in a valley
Elton: Anglo Saxon for Old Settlement
Erica: Latin for Heather
Ester, Hester: Persian for Myrtle
Glen, Glyn: Welsh for Valley
Hazel: After the tree
Heather: After the plant
Iris: Flower name
Ivy: After the plant
Jasmine: After the plant
Laura: After the Bay tree Laurel
Laurence: Associated with Laurel
Lee, Leigh: Old English for Meadow
Lily, Lillian: From the Latin for Flax
Marigold: Flower name
Olive, Olivia, Oliver: After the olive tree
Peter: The Rock
Quentin: Celtic for Hound of the Meadow
Rhoda, Rosalie, Rosaline, Rosamund, Rose: Associated
   with roses
Rosemary: Flower name
Ross: Gaelic meaning Of The Peninsular
Russell: The fox
Shelley: A wood
Shirley: A shire meadow
Silvia, Sylvia: Of the wood
Stanley: Stone field in Anglo Saxon
Susan: From the Hebrew for Lily
Viola, Violet: Flower name
Yasmine: Flower name

SATURN NAMES:
Bartholomew: Son of the Furrow – Saturn is the God of
   Agriculture
Constance, Constantine: Latin for Constancy
Fabian, Fabia: The grower
George: Farmer

Gregory: Watchful, watchman – Saturn is associated with timekeeping and the passage of time
Teresa: The reaper
Trevor: Discreet

FAMOUS CAPRICORNS:

Humphrey Bogart
Cary Grant
Ava Gardner
Howard Hughes
Mao Tse Tung
Richard Nixon
Albert Schweitzer
Susannah York
Rod Stewart
Bryan Robson

Des O'Connor
Anthony Andrews
Michael Aspel
Faye Dunaway
Princess Michael of Kent
Michael Crawford
Ted Willis
Lee Van Cleef
Peter Barkworth

AQUARIUS
20 January to 18 February

RULING PLANET: Uranus
ELEMENT: Air
GEMSTONE: Amethyst

Aquarius the water carrier is perhaps the most difficult sign of the Zodiac to characterize. Nothing about a little Aquarian is what it seems. Even the sign itself, which appears to relate to water, is more under the influence of Air.

Aquarians are puzzling, unpredictable, often infuriating to those who do not understand them. Their minds flit from one idea to another and they appear to lack concentration. What in fact is happening is that the Aquarian has so many things to think about in his bright, inventive way that more mundane considerations are often overlooked.

It is no surprise that they are called the geniuses of the Zodiac. The scope and potential of Aquarians is almost boundless. As children they may take up several different hobbies simultaneously and have equally diverse dreams and ambitions.

You never know how you stand with an Aquarian. Despite their inquiring minds working overtime, they can be absent-minded about everyday things, from tying shoelaces to combing their hair. Aquarians seem beyond their years, always one step ahead somewhere in the future, rather than having their feet firmly planted in the present.

At the same time they have no clear sense of direction. Plans switch, goals change, but always with the same bright flash of inspiration which rarely fails to impress.

Aquarian children are deeply affectionate but, to mum's dismay, find it difficult to express their love in physical hugs and kisses. This in no way diminishes their regard for parents and family.

Friends, however, are seen in a different perspective. Even as toddlers, Aquarians seldom settle for one or two close friends. Be prepared for gangs of casual acquaintances to invade your kitchen for snacks handed out by your generous February child.

Aquarians are quiet, loyal and fair-minded in ways which will make you feel proud of them. On the negative side they rarely respond to stern authority and, if you overlook their feelings, you may find you have a rebel in the house.

Intellectually, there are similar problems. If your Aquarian's intuition and flashes of problem-solving genius are steered in the right direction, you will be surprised. Should you, however, mistakenly think your little dreamer is not too bright, lack of stimulation may result in stubbornness, wilful behaviour and even eccentricity.

Life with an Aquarian is never easy, but it can be a wonderful challenge which will repay all your efforts.

AQUARIAN NAMES:
Ambrose: Ambrosia was originally regarded as the water of life – symbol of Aquarius the water carrier
Spencer: The dispenser
Valentine: St Valentine's Day falls in Aquarius

AIR NAMES:
Eve, Eva: From the Irish for Sunlight
Fay, Faye: Fairy, spirit of the air
Keith: Gaelic for the Wind
Lucian, Lucille, Lucy: Light
Melissa: Greek meaning a Bee

URANUS NAMES:
Abner: Father of light – Uranus was god of the heavens
Bridget: Strength – Uranus influences independence
Celeste: Heaven, heavenly
Elaine: Light, brightness

Esther: Star
Hugh, Hugo: Inspiration, a Uranus influence
Selina: Heaven
Stella: Star
Xavier: Bright

FAMOUS AQUARIANS:

Ronald Reagan
Paul Newman
Somerset Maugham
Abraham Lincoln
Jack Lemmon
Mia Farrow
Charles Dickens
Lewis Carroll
Lord Byron

Jeanne Moreau
Bill Gibb
Desmond Morris
Jools Holland
Eartha Kitt
Sacha Distel
Norman Mailer
Dennis Skinner
Germaine Greer

PISCES
19 February to 20 March

RULING PLANET: Neptune
ELEMENT: Water
GEMSTONE: Bloodstone

Pisceans are often regarded as perfect children. They seldom cry until they are red in the face, scream at nappy-changing time or tip their food dish upside down on the table. As babies they have a reputation for being the quietest and most content in the Zodiac nursery.

Before this picture becomes too rosy, it is worth considering the problems of the March child. Admittedly they are few, but you will notice that your little Piscean has a set of rules, quite different from your own. The timetable you carefully plan for feeding, bathtime and bed will soon go out of the window. Pisceans are regulated by an inner clock which makes them prefer to eat when they are hungry and sleep when they are tired.

In the early days this can be quite exhausting, and a gentle nudge towards regularity will not go amiss. In doing so you must not forget that Pisceans are perhaps the most sensitive and emotional sun sign. These loving children who inhabit their own dream world hate coercion of any kind.

They are extremely talented and creative, often becoming dancers, artists or writers. The driving force is their rich imagination which, even in childhood, has been known to display psychic tendencies. A Pisces child may surprise you by knowing what you are about to say before you say it.

Young Pisceans love make-believe – playing parts or acting out games with invented characters – and it is no surprise that many become actors. One point to remember is that because they live by their own rules and are dreamers by nature, they may bend their version of events to suit themselves if put on the spot. This does not necessarily mean that they are untruthful, or that they have the makings of an habitual liar. A little stretching of the facts helps a Piscean under pressure to avoid the real world, allowing more time to remain in a cocoon of dreams.

At their best – and that is the side Piscean children usually display – they can be delightfully selfless, deeply understanding of other people's feelings, sensitive and genuinely sympathetic. Misunderstanding, or a discordant home life may lead to a lack of confidence and vagueness. Take heart – it is unlikely to happen. You will feel blessed with a Piscean baby.

PISCES NAMES:

Barnabas, Barnaby: Son of consolation – a Piscean quality

Freda: Peaceful

Simon: From the Hebrew for Listening – a Piscean quality

Terence: Soft and tender

Wilfred: Peace in Old English

WATER NAMES:

Brook(e): Dweller at a watercourse

Doris, Dorise: Sea nymph

Douglas: A Celtic river

Dylan: Legendary sea god

Irving: Sea Friend in Old English

Kelvin: Gaelic for Narrow Stream

Lyn: Waterfall

Mary: Star of the sea

Mervyn, Marvin: Sea hill

Morgan: Seabright

Muriel: Sea

Murray: Sea, Sea Warrior in Celtic

Roland: Old Welsh for the Torrent

Rosemary: Dew of the sea

Winifred: Welsh for White Stream

NEPTUNE NAMES:
Meredith: Guardian of the sea
Norman: God of the Sea in Old German

FAMOUS PISCEANS:
Elizabeth Taylor
Lord Snowdon
John Steinbeck
Handel
Chopin
Michelangelo
Rudolf Nureyev
Vaslav Nijinsky
Auguste Renoir
Sidney Poitier
W.H. Auden

Jilly Cooper
Anton Mosimann
Anthony Burgess
Tom Courtney
Johnny Cash
Grace Kennedy
Shakin' Stevens
Eddy Grant
Micky Spillane
Michael Caine

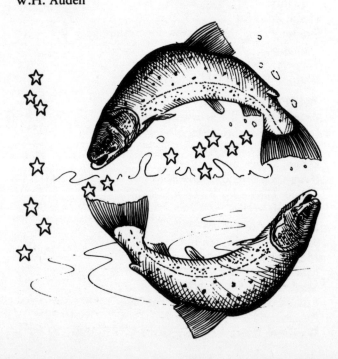

NAMES AND THEIR MEANINGS

A

Abigail (g) From the Hebrew for Father's Delight. A favourite name in biblical times and common in Britain in the seventeenth century. The name has been revived recently, mainly in its shortened forms Abby, Abbie and Gail.

Abel (b) Hebrew for Son or A Breath. In the Old Testament Abel was the second son of Adam and Eve.

Abraham (b) An obviously biblical name from the Hebrew meaning Father of Multitudes. Abraham Lincoln, sixteenth President of the USA, assassinated in 1865, led the North in the American Civil War to abolish slavery in the South. The name became synonymous with honesty because of Lincoln's reputation as a referee at cock-fights. Shortened forms of the name are Abe, Abie, Ham and Bram.

Adelaide (g) Other variations of this name are Adeline (remember the old song 'Sweet Adeline'?). Adela and its French form Adèle, all derived from Old German meaning Noble or Noble daughter.

Adrian (b) Derived from the Latin town Adria which gave its name to the Adriatic sea. Another form is Hadrianus, the Roman Emperor famous for the wall he built across Northern England. The only English pope, Nicolas Breakspeare (1154–1159) was titled Adrian IV.

Adriana (g) Other forms are Adrianne and Adrienne (French). The feminine form of Adrian.

Agnes (g) From the Greek meaning Pure or Chaste. Mostly associated with St Agnes, an early Christian martyr who, having consecrated her life to Christ, refused to marry the son of the prefect of Rome. Old

English superstitions about the Eve of St Agnes revealing the identity of future husbands probably arose around this time (third century). Variations include Annis, Annice, Annes and Agneta. In Scotland Nessie and Nessa, and in Wales, Nest and Nesta.

Alan (b) In Latin it means Cheerful, in Gaelic, Winsome and in Celtic, Harmony. Alwn Auleen was the brother of Bran the blessed. After the Norman Conquest the name became popular as Alain and Alein. Allan, Allen and Alun are other forms.

Alberta (g) Feminine form of Albert. Other variants include Albertine and Albertha.

Aldous (b) Old German meaning Old although another possible meaning is Awful Warrior. There were three eighth-century saints named Aldo and Aldous. Perhaps the most modern example is Aldous Huxley the English essayist and novelist (1894–1963) whose works included *Brave New World*.

Alec (b) Also spelt Aleck – both are shortened forms of Alexander, although often given as names in their own right.

Alessandra (g) The Italian spelling of the feminine form of Alexander from which the name Sandra is derived.

Alexandra (g) The feminine form of Alexander. Common to both Russia and Britain. Queen Victoria's son, the future King Edward VII, married the Danish Princess Alexandra in 1863. She founded the Queen Alexandra's Royal Army Nursing Corps. The name has retained much of its popularity and has continued in Royal use.

Alfred (b) Old English, Aelfraed, meaning Elf-Counsel. Another possible source is Old German where the meaning is Wise as a Supernatural Being. Celebrated Alfreds include Alfred Lord Tennyson the poet and Alfred Nobel who founded the Nobel Prize. In its shortened form Alfie, the film of the name starring Michael Caine, was a box office hit in the 1960s.

Alice (g) Old German derived from Adalheidis, meaning Noble Kind, and used as an ancient title for German princesses. The name was probably introduced into Britain by the Normans and has many variations: Allissa, Alicia, Alison – common in Scotland – and Alys the Welsh version. Alice is the most popular, especially after Lewis Carroll's *Alice in Wonderland* which has ensured its continued use up to present times.

Aline (g) A short form of Adeline which has become popular as an independent name. Other versions are Arleen and Arline.

Amelia (g) or Amelie comes from the Old German meaning worker. Another possible source is the Roman family name Aemilianus. The Hanoverian royal line introduced it to Britain where it became more popular as Emily, the name of George III's youngest daughter. Milly is a pet form.

Amy (g) From the French, meaning loved. Fashionable in the nineteenth century and revived by the famous airwoman Amy Johnson. Another form is Aimée.

Andrea (g) or Andree, the feminine form of Andrew.

Andrew (b) Greek meaning Manly or King. St Andrew was one of the first of Christ's disciples. Patron saint of Russia and Scotland where it has always been popular. Prince Andrew is Queen Elizabeth II's second son. Shortened forms include Andy and Drew.

Angus (b) Gaelic meaning One Choice. A national favourite in Scotland.

Ann, Anne, Anna (g) Generally supposed to come from the Hebrew name Hannah meaning Grace. Hannah was the mother of the prophet Samuel. St Anne is traditionally the mother of the Virgin Mary and is the patron saint of carpenters. Celebrated holders include, Anna Sewell who wrote *Black Beauty*, Queen Anne, Anne Boleyn, Anne of Cleves and more recently Princess Anne. There are many forms including Anita,

Annette, Anais, Annie, Anneka, Nan, Nanette, Nancy, Annemarie, etc.

Anthea (g) Greek meaning Lady of Flowers. Its diminutive is Thea.

Antony (b) Latin meaning Much Esteemed. Antonius was common among the Romans and Antonios was the Greek version meaning Flourishing. St Anthony the Great, an Egyptian (251–356), is regarded as the father of Christian monasticism. The 'h' which is often silent, was introduced after the Renaissance. Tony is the usual shortened form of the name.

Antonia (g) Feminine form of Antony. The French version Antoinette was made famous by the French Queen Marie Antoinette.

April (g) The name of the month, probably originating in the twentieth century. May be chosen to commemorate the time of birth. Other spellings include Avril and Averil.

Arabel, Arabella (g) Origins are obscure, possibly derived from Old German meaning Hilda's Eagle but more generally supposed to come from the Latin meaning Yielding to Prayer. Found in Scotland in the thirteenth century. Sometimes shortened to Belle or Bella.

Arthur (b) A name from legend, its sources are uncertain. There was a Roman family name Artorius, or it could come from the Celtic meaning Lofty a Stone. The old spelling was Artur. Arthur Wellesley, the Duke of Wellington, victor of the Battle of Waterloo gave the name impetus during the nineteenth century.

Austin (b) Derives from the Latin Augustine, meaning venerable or majestic. St Augustine was the first Archbishop of Canterbury. The femine forms Augusta and Augustine, though popular in Victorian times, seem to have fallen from favour today.

B

Barbara (g) Greek for Stranger and applied to those who did not speak their language. St Barbara was a third-century martyr.

Beatrice or Beatrix (g) From the Latin meaning Bringer of Blessings. Beatrix was the earlier version used by Dante, Shakespeare and Thackeray. Queen Victoria also chose it for her youngest daughter. Continuing its literary associations it is the name of the well known children's author and illustrator Beatrix Potter. Bea, Beatty and Trixie are the usual abbreviations.

Benedict (b) Latin meaning Blessed, another meaning is One Who Speaks Well, who says a benediction. In the fifth century, St Benedict founded the Benedictine Order of monks. Its most common diminutive is Ben.

Benjamin (b) From the Hebrew meaning Son of My Right Hand or Son of Strength. Ben or Benjy are the usual shortened forms.

Bernard (b) Has roots in Old German and Anglo-Saxon meaning Courageous Like a Bear. In the twelfth century, St Bernard of Clairvaux inspired the Second Crusade. St Bernard dogs are named after St Bernard of Menthon.

Bertram, Bertrand (b) Old German for Bright Raven, Bright House. Both names share the diminutives Bert, Bertie and less common, Berry.

Beverley (b) or (g) Sometimes spelled Beverly, from Anglo-Saxon meaning Beaver Meadow. Used firstly as a surname, it became a male Christian name and around the middle of this century was in vogue as a girl's Christian name.

Blair (b) This is an example of an Old Scottish surname which has been adopted as a Christian name. In Gaelic it means Battleground.

Bonnie (g) Latin origin meaning Good. Recently popularized by the all-round entertainer, Bonnie Langford. Alternative spelling: Bonny.

Boris (b) Russian for Warrior or Fight. Made famous by the film actor, Boris Karloff.

Brenda (g) Possibly Old Norse meaning Sword. It came into its own during the 1920s and 1930s, and is still quite common.

Brendan (b) Currently very popular in Britain and one of the top 50 names in Australia. Comes from the Irish Brenaian, meaning Dweller by the Beacon.

Bronwen (g) Sometimes related to legends and a popular name in Wales. Its Celtic meaning is White Breasted. Alternative spelling: Bronwyn.

Bruce (b) Initially introduced to Britain as a Scottish surname at the time of the Norman Conquest. Comes from the Old French, meaning Obscure. Although popular in Scotland, England and Australia, it has only been used as a Christian name since the nineteenth century.

Bruno (b) Rather an uncommon name originating from the Old German, meaning Brown or Swarthy. It was recently popularized by Radio One DJ, Bruno Brookes.

C

Cameron (b) Originating from the Gaelic meaning Crooked Nose, it is also the name of a famous Scottish clan. It is mainly used as a Christian name in Scotland, Australia and Canada.

Cara, Kara (g) Carey is another version of this name which comes from the Irish for Friend and also the Italian for Dear.

Carl, Karl (b) Karl is the German form of Charles. In America and Britain the name has been adopted and anglicized by spelling with a 'c'.

Carla (g) Derived from Caroline but now often used as a Christian name in its own right.

Carol, Carole (b) or (g) Its origins are rather obscure. It is generally supposed to be a feminine form of Charles derived from the Latin, Carolus. Another explanation is the Gaelic for Melody – is occasionally used as a boy's name in America.

Caroline, Carolyn (g) Another feminine form of Charles probably derived from Carolina, the Italian feminine form of Carlo. Pet names include Caro, Carrie and Lyn.

Catriona (g) A Gaelic form of Katharine and the title of a novel by Robert Louis Stevenson. The name is perhaps most popular in Scotland.

Cecil (b) Originally a surname, derived from the Latin Caecilius which was a Roman family name. Cecil was first adopted in Britain as a girl's Christian name. Nowadays it has fallen from favour and when used is generally supposed to be a boy's name.

Chantal, Chantelle (g) Borrowed from the French by many English speaking countries and popular in Canada.

Charles (b) From the Old English Ceorl and the Old German Carl, meaning Man or Manly. Made popular in France during the Middle Ages by the Emperor Charlemagne, the name came to Britain with the Normans in the twelfth century. The Royal House of Stuart favoured it throughout the seventeenth and eighteenth centuries and the Prince of Wales has ensured its continued use.

Charlotte (g) French feminine form of Charles introduced into Britain in the early seventeenth century. George III's wife was Charlotte Sophia, and George IV gave the name to his daughter. Perhaps the most famous Charlotte was the Brontë sister who wrote *Jane Eyre*. The name has maintained its popularity to the present day.

Christian (b) The name, popular with Scandinavian kings, has enjoyed a revival in modern times. Latin origin meaning Follower of Christ.

Christine, Christina (g) Also occasionally spelled Christiana. The name is the female form of Christian.

Christopher (b) Greek meaning Christ bearer. This was the title of the giant in the beautiful allegory who was ever in search of the strongest master. He found him at last in a little child whom he bore on his shoulders over a river. St Christopher, a deeply venerated martyr, became the patron saint of travellers. Chris and Kit are the most common abreviated forms.

Cindy (g) Derived from Lucinda or Cynthia. The shortened form, Cindy, has since become an independent name.

Clair, Claire, Clare, Clara (g) Latin origin for Bright, Clear and also Famous. St Clare, the thirteenth-century saint, was a disciple of St Francis of Assisi who founded the order of Franciscan nuns called the Poor Clares. Clara Schumann (1819–96) the German composer and concert pianist, Clara Bow the American film star who thrilled the flapper generation and more recently British film actress Claire Bloom have contributed to the name's popularity.

Clarence (b) The male version of Clare, generally supposed to mean Famous.

Clarice, Clarissa (g) Two more versions of Clair.

Clark, Clarke (b) A surname adopted as a Christian name. From Old English meaning Clergyman or Learned Man, Author or Reader. American heart-throb Clark Gable and, of course, Clark Kent alias Superman, popularized the name during the latter half of this century.

Claud (b) Greek meaning Famous, and also the Latin for

Lame. Claudius was a Roman family name introduced to Britain by the Emperor Claudius.

Claudia (g) Female version of Claud, popular in France and America. Other forms include Claudette and Claudine.

Cleo (g) Strictly speaking this name is derived from Cleopatra the famous Egyptian queen. Her name, immortalized by Shakespeare, is as familiar today as it was in 30 BC. Originally Greek, meaning Glory, or Father's Fame.

Clive (b) A modern name, probably derived from Clifford. It was made famous by Robert Clive, or Clive of India, as he was known. Adopted as a Christian name and popular with those who had connections with India.

Colin (b) Celtic for Noble Wolf, Gaelic meaning A Young dog or Youth, also from the French Nicholas, and in Scotland derived from the missionary St Columba. It was a family name of the Campbells and has spread into wide use across Britain.

Constantine (b) The male version of Constance from the Latin meaning Firm. It is also possibly from the Celtic for Friendship. Popular with Christians from early times. Three Scottish kings were named Constantine after a Cornish saint from the sixth century who was believed to have converted their ancestors to Christianity.

Courtney (b) or (g) Probably derived from a French placename. A surname adopted as a Christian name and popularized by young Londoner Courtney Pine, one of the world's leading jazz saxophonists.

Crispin, Crispian (b) Latin meaning Curled. St Crispin is the patron saint of shoemakers.

Cyril (b) From the Greek for Lord. In the ninth century, St Cyril introduced Christianity to the Slavs and devized the Cyrillic alphabet. There is a rare feminine form, Cyrilla.

D

Damian, Damien (b) A typical example of an old name which has become a 'new' name from the Greek meaning Tamer. There have been four saints of this name. More recently the name was used in the film *The Omen*, in which the boy was supposed to be Satan.

Danielle (g) French female form of Daniel. Also increasing in popularity, especially in Canada.

David (b) Hebrew for Beloved. In the Old Testament David killed Goliath and later became the second king of Israel. In the sixth century Dawfydd, a Welshman of princely birth, was Archbishop of Menevia. He was deeply venerated and made the patron saint of Wales. The name has been in common use both as a Christian name and the basis of many surnames in Britain since the twelfth century.

Davina (g) A feminine form of David which is most popular in Scotland. An alternative is Davida, but this is quite rare.

Dawn (g) A fairly modern name which came into vogue in the late nineteenth century. It is the English version of the Latin name Aurora, meaning Daybreak.

Dean (b) Old German, meaning Dweller in a Valley. A surname which became adopted as a Christian name. Celebrated examples include the late James Dean, the 1950s' screen idol who became a cult figure, and movie star Dean Martin.

Deborah (g) Hebrew meaning Bee. An Old Testament name of a prophetess. The Puritans favoured the name in the seventeenth century and it has enjoyed some popularity over the past 20 years. Debra is a modern spelling and its diminutives are Deb and Debbie.

Deirdre (g) Celtic meaning Raging One. 'Deirdre of the sorrows' was a legendary figure who left Ireland to marry the man she loved. When he and his two brothers were tempted back and killed, Deirdre in her sorrow committed suicide. The name was popularized by Irish poetry.

Denise (g) The feminine form of Denis which was popular in the 1950s and 1960s.

Derek, Deric, Derick, Derrick (b) Derived from the Old German, Theodoric meaning Ruler of the People. Two Saxon names Theodric and Tedrick are recorded in the Domesday book. Deryk came to Britain around the fifteenth century but only became popular in the last century.

Dermot (b) This is the anglicized spelling of the ancient Irish name Diarmuit who was famous in legend as the lover of Grainne, Queen of Tara. The name, meaning Free Man, is most common in Ireland.

Desmond (b) Originally a Celtic clan name meaning From South Munster. A surname that was adopted as a Christian name around the nineteenth century.

Diana, Diane (g) Roman goddess of the hunt and protector of wild animals, goddess of light, the moon and virginity. Diane, the French form, was fashionable during the Renaissance and the Princess of Wales has made the name a popular choice today. Variations include, Dyan and Dyanna.

Dick (b) The shortened form of Richard, now sometimes used as a name in its own right.

Dirk (b) The Dutch form of Derek. Dirk Bogart, the film actor, has widened its use in English speaking countries.

Dominic(k) (b) Latin meaning Born on the Lord's Day. In England before the Norman Conquest it was predominantly a monk's name. St Dominic founded the thirteenth-century Order of Preachers in Spain, which became the Dominican Order. The feminine forms Dominica and Dominique are rarely found in England.

Donald (b) Gaelic derived from Domhnall, meaning Ruler of the World. Popular in the Highlands and also as Donal in Ireland.

Donna (g) The Italian word for Lady was adopted as a Christian name during the last century and is most popular in North America.

Dora (g) Originally a contraction of Dorothy or Theodora, Dora became an independent name during the nineteenth century. William Wordsworth, the poet, called his daughter Dora.

Doreen (g) Most popular before World War II. The name comes from the Irish, Doirean, which was probably adapted from Dorothy.

Dorothea, Dorothy (g) Greek, meaning Gift of God. The name has been used in Britain since the fifteenth century, often in its shortened form, Dolly. It is popularly supposed that this is how dolls received their name. Most celebrated examples are Dorothy L. Sayers creator of the fictional detective, Lord Peter Wimsey, and Dorothy, the little heroine from *The Wizard of Oz*. Short forms include, Dora, Dot, Dottie, Dodo and Dodie.

Dougal, Dugald (b) Dubh gall is Old Irish for Black Stranger and was used by the Irish to describe the Norwegians, and later the English. It was adopted by the Scots as a Christian name and is still commonly found in the Highlands.

Dudley (b) A distinguished Tudor surname. Robert Dudley, Earl of Leicester was a courtier to Elizabeth I. Dudley was adopted as a Christian name in the nineteenth century.

Duke (b) Originally a shortened form of Marmaduke. Duke was also a nick name originating from the title. It has now become an independent name popularized by Duke Ellington, the celebrated jazz pianist.

Dwayne, Duane (b) Origins obscure, possibly adopted from an Irish surname.

E

Edgar (b) Old English meaning Happy or Fortunate Spear. Edgar was at its most popular during the nineteenth century. Edgar Wallace the celebrated crime writer (1875–1932) is perhaps the best-known recent holder.

Edward (b) A proud Old English name which has stood the test of time and remained a favourite down the centuries. Three King Edwards succeeded Alfred the Great. St Edward (Edward the Confessor) was the last Saxon king to reign peacefully. Henry III named his sons Edmund and Edward and the name survived the Norman Conquest. There have been eight other King Edwards, the last being Edward VIII who abdicated in 1936 in order to marry Mrs Ernest Simpson. An ancient and celebrated Edward was the Black Prince (1330–1376) and a more recent example, Edward Heath, Conservative Prime Minister in 1970.

Eileen, Aileen (g) Generally considered to be the Irish form of Helen which became familiar throughout Britain in the twentieth century.

Eleanor (g) Introduced to England by Eleanor of Aquitaine, wife of Henry II in the twelfth century. Henry III's wife was Queen Eleanor of Provence. Edward I's first wife, Eleanor of Castile, accompanied him on the crusades where she is reputed to have saved his life by sucking poison from a wound. The name gained favour after her death when Edward erected 'Eleanor Crosses' at all the places where her *cortège* had rested. The name is a variant of Helen and other forms include, Eleanora, Eleanore, Elinor and Ellenor.

Eliot, Elliot (b) Origin obscure but generally supposed to be derived from Elias and Elijah, popular in the Middle Ages. Originally, Eliot was used as a surname but has since been adopted as a Christian name.

Elizabeth (g) Hebrew, Elisheba, meaning God Hath Sworn. There is also a Greek source, Elisabet, and the Latin, Elizabetha. It was used as a Christian name in the Eastern Church and brought to Europe. In France it had the form Isabel, which was also found in medieval England. Elizabeth became firmly established during the long reign of Elizabeth I and has retained its popularity through to our present Queen Elizabeth II. There are many variants and diminutives including, Bess, Bessie, Bet, Beth, Betsy, Betty, Elsbet, Elspeth, Elsa, Eliza, Libby, Lilibet, Lilibeth, Lisbeth, Liz, Lizzie, Lizzy, Lisa, Liza.

Ellen (g) Another form of Helen.

Elmer (b) The name is derived from Aylmer of the Old English Ethelmer and means Noble.

Elroy (b) Clearly derived from the French for The King, the name is also from the Latin for Regal.

Elsa, Elsie (g) Both names are contractions of Elizabeth.

Elvira (g) A name with literary connections. Elvira was the heroine of Victor Hugo's *Hernani* and the deceased first wife in Noel Coward's *Blithe Spirit*.

Emily (g) This is the most popular feminine form of Emile which comes from the Latin family name of Aemilius. The name is understood to mean Industrious. There are many forms including Amelia, the name given to George II's daughter who was known as Princess Emily, Emelye, the version used by Chaucer, Emelia and Emmeline.

Emma (g) Old German in origin and meaning Universal. The name has a charming history. The first Emma we know of was a daughter of Charlemagne who was said to have carried her lover over the snow so that his footprints would not betray his visits. Perhaps the most famous Emma was the heroine of Jane Austen's novel of the same name. Its publication in the early nineteenth century made the name one of the most fashionable of the time.

Eric (b) Norse meaning Ever King. Eric is the name of several Swedish and Danish kings. It was brought to Britain by the Danes, but its use was spasmodic until the nineteenth century. Since then it has become an established name in Britain.

Ethel (g) A name with an ancient lineage. Ethel has fallen out of vogue, but like many old names continues in familiar usage until its star rises again. From Anglo-Saxon aethel, meaning Noble, Ethel was the root of names such as Ethelred and Ethelinda. During the nineteenth century it became an independent name and was used by Thackeray in *The Newcomers*.

Evan, Ewan (b) Other spellings include Euan and Ewen. Greek and Welsh in origin, meaning Youth Warrior. Generally supposed to be the Welsh and Scottish forms of John.

Evelyn, Eveline (b) or (g) In the twelfth century the Normans brought the Old German name Aveline to England where it was used as a surname. Another possible source is the Irish Eveleen. Eveline was developed into a Christian name from which Evelyn, the more modern form, evolved.

F

Faith (g) From the Latin Fides. Fides Publica was the Roman goddess who represented the people's honour. Her feast day was celebrated on 1 October. Faith is one of the virtue names adopted by the Puritans during the sixteenth and seventeenth centuries. Unlike some of their more extreme examples, Faith has remained in common usage.

Felicity (g) Other forms include Felicia and Felice. From the Latin for Happiness it is the female form of Felix.

Felix (b) Latin meaning Happy and Gaelic meaning The Ever Good. In Ireland the name is adapted to Feidlim or Phelim.

Fenella (g) Known in Britain during the nineteenth century after Scott's novel *Peveril of the Peak* its meaning comes from the Irish for White and Shoulder. Finola is a variation.

Fergus (b) Celtic meaning Man of Virtue or Man of Action. Widespread in Scotland, Ireland and the North of England.

Fiona (g) The name, from the Gaelic for Fair, was introduced as the pseudonym Fiona Macleod, by William Sharp in the nineteenth century in his mystical Celtic writings. It has become increasingly popular and has many variants including Fionola, Fionnuala and Fionnula.

Florence (g) Formerly both a male and female name from the Latin meaning Blooming. In honour of Florence Nightingale, and the famous Italian town, the name enjoyed a considerable vogue in the nineteenth century.

Floyd (b) From the Welsh name Lloyd. Widespread in America and popularized by Floyd Patterson, the former heavyweight boxing champion.

Frances (g) From the Italian Francesco. Francesca, the feminine form, and Françoise the French feminine form were introduced around the thirteenth century. By Tudor times, Frances was adopted by the English aristocracy. The name has remained in general use, though it is becoming more rare.

Francis (b) From the Latin for Frenchman and the Old German for Free Lord. Francis has at least two celebrated historical namesakes, St Francis of Assisi and Sir Francis Drake. Although not common in this country until around the sixteenth century, the name has continued in general use since then. Variants include Frank and Frankie.

Frank (b) A variant of Francis which has become accepted as a name in its own right. The best example is probably movie star and singer Frank Sinatra.

Frederick (b) Old German for Warrior of Peace or Peaceful Ruler. The name George II gave to his eldest son spread throughout the Hanoverian reign to become one of the most popular boys' names of the nineteenth century.

G

Gail (g) A contraction of Abigail which has been recognized as a separate name for some time. Gale and Gayle are alternative spellings.

Gareth (b) Generally supposed to come from the Welsh meaning Gentle. Gareth is probably a variant of Gerard. Mallory used the name in *Morte d'Arthur* in the sixteenth century and Tennyson in the nineteenth century included his poem 'Gareth and Lynette' in his *Idylls of the King*. Now in regular use, especially in Wales. Variants include, Gary and Garth.

Gary (b) A variant of Gareth which has been accepted as an independent name.

Gavin, Gawain (b) Sir Gawain is one of the best known Knights of the Round Table in Arthurian legend. Occasionally referred to as Walwain there could be a link with the Old English name Walwyn, meaning Friend in Battle. It is, however, generally accepted to be a Welsh name meaning Hawk of May. Gavin, thought to be a French form, is often used in Scotland.

Gay, Gaye (g) A modern name taken from the adjective meaning happy, cheery, etc.

Gemma (g) Italian for Gem. Actress Gemma Craven is probably the best example of this uncommon name.

Geoffrey, Jeffrey (b) Old German meaning Divine Peace. During the twelfth century Geoffrey of Monmouth, a Benedictine monk, created the romantic legend of King Arthur. Geoffrey Chaucer, author of *The Canterbury Tales*, was the first poet to be buried in Poet's Corner after his death in 1400. The name is found in many forms in surnames such as Jeffries, Jeeves, Jepson. Geoff and Jeff are the most common abbreviations.

Georgina (g) Feminine form of George which first appeared as Georgina during the eighteenth century. During the nineteenth century Georgiana became the accepted version which is still in use today. Georgette, the French form, is also found in English speaking countries as an unusual Christian name.

Geraldine (g) Still fairly common today, the name simply means One of the Fitzgeralds. It was introduced by Tudor poet Henry Howard, Earl of Surrey in a poem about Lady Elizabeth Fitzgerald, whom he addressed as the 'Fair Geraldine'.

Gervais (b) Originally from Old German meaning War Like Eagerness, Gervais is the Old Norman form. During the twelfth century the name was used by the English clergy in honour of the first-century martyr St Gervase. Its use spread giving rise to the surname Jarvis. Alternate spellings include Gervaise, Jervais and Jervis.

Gilbert (b) A Norman name which came to Britain with the Conquest and means Bright Pledge. The name has been used as a basis for many surnames such as Gibbs, Gibson and Gibbons.

Gillian, Jillian (g) An English feminine form of the Latin Julian. Common during the Middle Ages when the short forms Gill and Jill were also used. The name enjoyed a revival in the middle of this century but has now become more scarce. Pet names include Gilly or Jilly.

Gladys (g) A Welsh name, from Gwladys, which became widespread and very popular during the nineteenth century. The name is still used though it has been out of fashion for some time.

Glenda, Glennis (g) Glenda Jackson is a famous example of a name which is probably a feminine form of Glenn, first introduced in America during the nineteenth century. There is however another explanation accepted by some as Welsh meaning Holy Good.

Glynis (g) The feminine form of Glyn, found almost exclusively in Wales.

Godfrey (b) Originally Old German; the Norman form meaning Divine Peace came to England with the Conquest. There was also an Old English name Godfrith but Godfrey was the form that survived.

Gordon (b) A place in Scotland from which the local lords took their name and founded the powerful Gordon Clan. The surname was adopted as a Christian name after the death of General Gordon of Khartoum at the end of the nineteenth century, and came into general use in England and Scotland.

Grace (g) Like many other charmingly old-fashioned names, Grace is enjoying a new popularity. From the Latin for Thanks, it is one of the virtue names that were favoured by the Puritans. The 1950s' star Grace Kelly, later Princess Grace of Monaco, is one of the most celebrated examples.

Graham, Graeme, Grahame (b) A surname which, like Gordon, was connected with a placename and adopted by a well-known Scottish family. During the present century it has been generally recognized as a Christian name and its use has become widespread.

Grant (b) Old French meaning Big or Great. Originally a surname which also became a middle name when the mother's maiden name was retained, and from that, was adopted as a christian name.

Guy (b) The Normans brought the name to Britain and it

appears in old records both as Wido, which is Old German, and Guido in Latin, the French form of which was Guy. The name fell out of favour after the Gunpowder Plot but was restored to use in the nineteenth century and popularized by Sir Walter Scott's novel, *Guy Mannering*.

Gwen, Gwenda (g) Feminine forms of Gwyn which are no longer used exclusively in Wales. Gwen is also a shortened form of Gwendoline but is now considered a name in its own right.

Gwyn (b) or (g) A masculine name in Wales meaning White or Fair, the name is the basis of many names including Gwen and the anglicized Wyn or Wynne.

Gwyneth (g) Welsh from Gwynedd meaning Blessed or Happy.

H

Hamish (b) Generally accepted as an anglicized form of the Gaelic Seamus or Seumas, equivalent to James. The name was favoured during the Victorian Era and is still in general use in Scotland.

Hannah (g) The name of Samuel's mother in the Old Testament, Hannah is a Hebrew name meaning Favour, Mercy or Grace. The Greek form Anna was the version used in England until the Reformation when Hannah, the original name, was adopted. It was popular during the Victorian Era and is now enjoying another revival.

Harriet (g) A feminine version of Henry, from the French Henriette. Introduced to England by Henrietta Maria, wife of Charles I. Anglicized to Harriot or Harriet, it became very popular during the eighteenth and nineteenth centuries.

Harry (b) An anglicized version of Henri and also a short form of Harold and a pet form of Henry. Now a favourite modern choice especially since the birth of Prince Harry, second son of Prince Charles and Princess Diana. Diminutive, Hal.

Heather (g) Another of the Victorian floral names which has endured and is still popular today.

Helen, Helena (g) A name that has stood the test of time. Helena the fourth-century saint, mother of Constantine the Great, made the pilgrimage to the Holy Land where it is said she found the true cross of Christ. In Greek the name means Light or The Bright One, and the legendary Helen of Troy helped to immortalize it. There are many variations and diminutives including Lena, Eleanor, Ellen and Ellie.

Henry (b) An Old German name meaning Home Ruler, which came to England at the time of the Norman Conquest and which has been in general and royal use ever since. There are too many famous Henrys to list but perhaps the best-known is Henry VIII.

Herbert (b) The name only became generally used after the Norman Conquest. Originally from Old German meaning Bright Army, its popularity during Victorian times may have something to do with the fashion for adapting aristocratic surnames into Christian names. Now fairly uncommon, it is still one of the oldest surnames in England.

Hilary, Hillary (g) or (b) The name came to England in the Middle Ages from France. St Hilary of Poitiers in the fourth century was a strong supporter of Christianity. From the Latin, it means Cheerful. It is only during this century that it has become more common as a girl's name.

Hilda (g) Old German meaning Battlemaid. In Scandinavian legend it was the name of the chief of the Valkyries. The seventh-century St Hilda founded Whitby Abbey in Yorkshire and during the nineteenth century, when many Anglo-Saxon saints' names were reused, Hilda enjoyed a revival. The name is still in general use today.

Howard (b) A family name of the Dukes of Norfolk which dates back to the thirteenth century and was adopted by the general public as a Christian name during the nineteenth century. Its origins are obscure with varied possible sources – Old German meaning Heart or Soul Protection, Old French for Osprey or Sword Guardian or an adaptation of Hayward, Harward, Hereward, etc.

Humphrey (b) Humfrey, was an aristocratic Old English name which possibly came from the Old English name Hunfrith or from the Old German meaning Giant Peace. It was adopted into general use and reached its popularity during the nineteenth century. Film star Humphrey Bogart who starred in *The Maltese Falcon* and *Casablanca* helped popularize the name in this century.

I

Ian, Iain (b) The Scottish form of John which became generally popular all over Britain during this century.

Imogen (g) The name of Shakespeare's heroine in *Cymberline* and popularly believed to be a misprint of the name Innogen, which in Old Irish (as 'ingen') means Daughter or Girl.

Ingrid (g) Meaning Ing's Ride. In Norse mythology Ing, god of fertility, rode a golden boar. Only recently used in Britain, probably due to the popularity of film star Ingrid Bergman.

Irene (g) Name of the ancient Greek goddess of peace. Irene only became generally used in England during the latter part of the nineteenth century and the early part of this century. The name can be pronounced with either two or three syllables.

Isaac (b) Son of Abraham and Sarah in the Bible. The name, which in Hebrew means Laughter, came into general use during the sixteenth and seventeenth centuries and was often spelt with a 'z' as in Izaak Walton, author of *The Compleat Angler*. Sir Isaac Newton, the scientist, used the 's' spelling. The name is now regarded as Jewish.

Isabel, Isobel, Isabella (g) A variant of Elizabeth which possibly originated in medieval France. Spanish Queen Isabella I was the patroness of Christopher Columbus. Like Elizabeth, the name has various diminutives including, Isa, Bella and Ibby.

Ivan (b) The Russian form of John occasionally found in Britain.

Ivor, Ifor (b) Ivor is generally accepted as the anglicized spelling of the Welsh name Ifor which means Lord. Ivor Novello, composer and dramatist, wrote the popular World War I song, *Keep The Home Fires Burning*.

J

Jack (b) A diminutive of John which by the Middle Ages was so common that it became an independent name. Jock is the Scottish variant.

Jacqueline (g) French feminine form of Jacques, which itself is the French form of Jacob and James. Although introduced into this country during the thirteenth century, it is only during the present century that the name has become widespread. Short forms include Jackie and Jacky.

James (b) Originally interchangeable with Jacob, James is accepted as the anglicized form. The name has strong biblical and royal associations including the apostle St James the Great and seven kings of Scotland, including James I and James II of England. Variations include Jim, Jimmy and Scottish forms Jamie and Hamish.

Jane, Jayne (g) Along with Joan and Joanne this name is one of the feminine forms of John and derived from the Old French Jehane. Jane Seymour, third wife of Henry VIII and mother of Edward VI, later Lady Jane Grey, established the name during Tudor times. It has remained popular with Janie, Janey and Jenny as its pet forms. Sine (English spelling, Sheena) is the Gaelic form.

Janet (g) Another of the feminine forms of John which first evolved in Scotland from the French Jeanette, a derivation of the Old French Jehane. Originally regarded as a Scottish diminutive, it has long since become a separate name with widespread usage. Pet names include, Jenny, Jan, Netta and Netty.

Janice (g) A modern form of Jane most popular around the middle of this century.

Jean, Jeanna, Jeanne, Jeannette (g) Like Jane, these names have also evolved from the Old French root name Jehane. Originally regarded as Scottish forms, they have long since passed into general use throughout Britain.

Jennifer, Jenny (g) The Old Cornish form of Guenevere and the name of King Arthur's wife, from the Welsh meaning Fair and Yielding. The name was revived around the middle of this century and has been popular and widespread ever since. The pet form Jenny is often used as an independent name. Others include Jen and Jennie.

Jeremy (b) English form of Jeremiah, name of the Old Testament prophet who wrote the *Book of Lament-*

ations. English usage dates back to the thirteenth century. Jerry is the usual shortened form.

Jessica (g) Hebrew meaning God Beholds. Jessica was the beautiful daughter of Shylock in Shakespeare's *The Merchant of Venice* which popularized the name. It has had continued use and is enjoying a modern revival, especially in America and Canada.

Jill, Jillian (g) see Gillian.

Joan (g) English feminine form of John. From Jhone or Johan, the French feminine form of the Latin Johannes, which was introduced here during the twelfth century. By the fourteenth century the English form, Joan, had become established. During the sixteenth century the name had become so common that it became unfashionable and was replaced by Jane, only to be revived as a popular choice at the beginning of this century.

Joanna, Johanna, Joanne (g) A feminine form of John, originally Hebrew meaning Grace of God. Johanna was the medieval Latin feminine form of Johannes (now John). The modern version, Joanne has taken over from Joan and is a popular choice.

Joe (b) Often used as an independent name, Joe is a diminutive of Joseph.

Joel (b) A Scripture name popular with the Puritans. Its origins are Hebrew, meaning Jehovah Is God. Still in regular use in America, the name is now arousing new interest in Britain.

John (b) As the name of Christ's cousin, John the Baptist, and also the disciple St John the Divine, it is hardly surprising that the name was a favourite with the Eastern Church. From the Hebrew meaning Jehovah Is Gracious, it was brought to Britain by the Crusaders and has been one of the most popular Christian names in Britain since the twelfth century. Other forms include the Gaelic Ian and Iain, the Welsh Evan and the Irish Sean.

Jonathan (b) Hebrew meaning Gift of God. Favoured by the Puritans because of its biblical associations, it has aroused new interest in recent times and is beginning to supercede the ever popular John.

Joseph (b) Hebrew meaning The Lord Added. In the Bible Rachel called her long awaited child Joseph. He was sold into slavery in Egypt by his brothers where he became a man of high rank able to help his family during the famine. Other biblical Josephs include the husband of Mary, mother of Jesus, and Joseph of Arimathea, who donated the tomb for Jesus's burial and is connected by legend to Glastonbury.

Josephine (g) The feminine form of Joseph and the name of Napoleon's first wife, the Empress Josephine, who popularized the name in both Britain and France. Diminutives include Jo and Josie.

Joy (g) The name dates back to the twelfth century and is simply taken from the Latin meaning Joy. A favourite with the Puritans and revived in the nineteenth century, it has remained in general use ever since.

Joyce (g) Originally a name for both sexes, it has been used as a girl's name only since the fourteenth century. In medieval times it took the form of Josse or the French form Joisse, from which Joyce was derived. The name peaked around 1925 and has since settled into regular use.

Judith (g) Hebrew meaning A Jewess. An ancient name first appearing in the Bible as the wife of Esau. The name reached England in the ninth century and after 1700, when Punch and Judy were introduced, Judy became the accepted diminutive. The name was used enthusiastically around the middle of this century owing to the popularity of film star Judy Garland.

Julia (g) The Latin feminine form of Julius. Shakespeare used the name Julia in *Two Gentlemen of Verona*. The name came into general use in the eighteenth century and has maintained a regular following. Julie is the

French form, while Juliet is generally supposed to come from Giulietta, the Italian version of Julia, adapted to Juliet and also used by Shakespeare.

Julian (b) From the Latin Julianus which is derived from the Roman clan name Julius. It is the name of many saints, including St Julian the Hospitaller who devoted himself to helping poor travellers as a penance for accidentally killing his own parents.

K

Karen (g) The Danish form of Katherine which came to Britain via America, reaching its peak in the 1960s.

Kate (g) A favourite form of Katherine popular in the sixteenth, seventeenth and nineteenth centuries, and which has long been accepted as an independent name.

Katharine, Katherine (g) see Catherine. Pet names include Kay or Kaye and Katie or Katy which have become accepted as names in their own right. Also Kathy and Kitty.

Kenneth (b) Kenneth MacAlpine was the first King of Scotland in the ninth century who succeeded in uniting the Picts and the Scots. Originally Scottish, from the Gaelic Coinneach meaning Handsome, the name spread and lost its strictly Scottish associations. The Welsh form is Cenydd and the Irish Canice. In vogue during the 1920s, the name has since maintained steady use.

Kerry, Kerrie, Kerie, Keri (b) or (g) From the Irish placename, also Celtic meaning Dark One. Originally a man's name, it was adapted as a girl's name becoming immensely popular in recent years, especially in Australia.

Kevin (b) From the Gaelic Caoin meaning Kind or Fair. St Kevin was a sixth-century hermit who became Abbot of Glendalough, a well known beauty spot in Ireland. During this century the name has become a firm favourite in Britain, America and Canada.

Kimberley, Kimberly (b) or (g) A modern name which probably originated as a surname after the South African town. Now generally recognized as a girl's Christian name, it is a favourite in America and is often found as Kim elsewhere.

Kirsten (g) A Scottish variant of the Scandinavian name Christiana or Christine, mostly used by families with Scottish associations. Alternative spellings include Kirstin and Kirsteen. The pet form is Kirsty.

Kirsty (g) The pet form of Kirsten, which has spread to most English speaking countries where it has become a popular name in its own right.

L

Leslie, Lesley (b) or (g) Originally an Aberdeenshire placename which was adopted as a surname by the Lords of Leslie and began to be used as a Christian name around the end of the nineteenth century. The masculine spelling is Leslie, which was very popular in the 1920s. Lesley, the feminine spelling, became a favourite during the 1960s, though it is less common today.

Lindsay, Lindsey (b) or (g) Originally an Old English place-name, probably Lindon, the old name for Lincoln. It was taken as a Scottish surname and later adapted as a Christian name. Now widely used as a girl's name with various spellings including Linsay and Linsey.

Lisa, Lisette, Liz, Liza see Elizabeth.

Lois (g) Probably Greek and occurs in the New Testament. An Old German source means Praise and Fame. One of the many biblical names used by the Puritans, and also considered by some as a variant form of Louise. Lois Lane, Superman's girlfriend is probably the most famous example.

Lorna (g) Introduced by R.D. Blackmore in his novel *Lorna Doone* published in 1869, the success of which no doubt popularized the name, for it has been in steady use ever since. Possibly taken from the Old English word 'lorn', as in forlorn, or from the place-name Lorne, as used in the title Marquis of Lorne.

Lorraine, Loraine (g) Old German meaning Famous Warrior, and a French place-name adopted as a Christian name. The name spread to America and Britain where it has been quite successful since the middle of this century.

Louisa, Louise (g) The Latin and French feminine forms of Louis. Louisa May Alcott, the American author of the celebrated classic *Little Women*, is one famous example, although both spellings are equally popular.

Lucy (g) From Lucia the feminine version of Lucius, meaning Light. The Romans often gave the name to children born at dawn or first light. The name with its many variations spread throughout Britain in Norman times but the simple anglicized form, Lucy, has remained the most popular, especially today when a nostalgia for Victorian favourites guides many parents' choice.

Luke (b) Another up and coming old name, from the Greek meaning Man of Luciana. St Luke the Evangelist, who recorded the life of St Paul, was called the 'beloved physician' and is the patron saint of doctors and painters. Lucas, the Latin form, was anglicized to Luke after the twelfth century and recognized as a family name for craftsmen.

M

Madeline, Magdalen (g) Hebrew meaning Woman of Magdala, birthplace of St Mary Magdalene. The French form, Madeline, was used in England from around the twelfth century. Although Magdalen, the biblical form, was introduced after the Reformation, Madeline remains as the most popular choice. Short forms include, Maddy, Maddie, Magda which is sometimes given as an independent name, and Madge, which is shared with Margaret.

Malcolm (b) Gaelic meaning Servant of St Columbia. There were four Scottish Kings of this name, the second of which was the persecutor of Lady Macbeth's family and the third, Duncan's grandson, who began assimilation with the English.

Mandy (g) The short form of Amanda and Miranda sometimes used as an independent name.

Margaret (g) Greek meaning A Pearl, and also Child of Light, which derives from the Persian term, Mervarid. This comes from a belief that oysters, rising to the surface at night, opened their shells in adoration and received drops of dew congealed by moonbeams into pearls – the pure, pale lustre of which resembles the moon. Some people call them 'tears of the moon'. St Margaret of Antioch, a third-century martyr, and the wife of Malcolm III, another St Margaret, who introduced the name into Scotland during the eleventh century, both influenced its popularity. Quite common in medieval England and during Victorian times, it is still an established favourite today. Variations and diminutives include, Madge, Meg, Peg, Peggy and Megan, the Welsh form. Maisie and Maggie are Scottish variants. Marguerite is the French form and also the name of the large white daisy-like flower – which is why Daisy is used as a pet form for Margaret.

Margery, Marjorie (g) Originally pet forms of Marguerite, the French form of Margaret, which was established as an independent name as early as the twelfth century. Although Marjorie was the Scottish variant it is now the most widely accepted spelling.

Margot, Marguerite (g) see Margaret.

Marian, Marion (g) From Marie, the French version of Mary, which was established as an independent name during medieval times. Robin Hood was in love with Maid Marian and the stories have popularized the name down the centuries. Marian and the French Marianne are later forms of Marion.

Marilyn (g) A version of Mary, established as an independent name. The most celebrated holder is probably the legendary screen star Marilyn Monroe.

Marlene, Marlena (g) A contraction of Magdalene. See Madeline. Made popular around the 1950s by film star Marlene Dietrich.

Marvin (b) see Mervyn.

Matthew (b) Hebrew meaning Gift of the Lord. St Matthew was a tax collector in the service of the Romans before he became a disciple of Christ. The Latin form is Matthaeus, the French, Matheu and the Greek Matthias. The name is mentioned in the Domesday Book and has remained in popular and regular use over the centuries up to the present when it remains as much a favourite as ever. Matt, Matty and Mattie are the usual shortened forms.

Maureen (g) A twentieth-century name from Mairin, a diminutive of Maire the Irish form of Mary.

May, Mae, Mai (g) This name represents the month and is sometimes chosen for this reason. It is also the diminutive of Mary and Margaret and, as such, is often regarded as a separate name. Mae and Mai are variant spellings made popular by actresses Mae West and Mai Britt.

Melanie (g) Greek meaning Dark or Black. The name

was used by both the Greeks and the Romans, and the French form, Melanie, became popular in the south-west of England during the seventeenth century.

Melinda (g) Origin obscure but generally supposed to be from the Greek meaning Sweet Soft. Names ending with 'inda' were popular in Stuart times, which is probably when the name was introduced.

Melvin, Melvyn (b) Origin obscure, but possible sources include Celtic meaning Chief; Gaelic, from Malvin meaning Smooth Brow; a place-name, or the Old English Maelwine meaning Sword or Speech Friend. Television personality and author, Melvyn Bragg is a well-known example.

Mervyn, Marvin (b) Old English from Maerwine meaning Famous Friend, or old Welsh from Myrddin, meaning Sea-hill, which is the true form of Merlin, King Arthur's legendary magician. Marvin is the American adaptation.

Michael (b) Hebrew meaning Who Is Like The Lord? Michael was one of the seven Archangels who defeated Satan in the *Book of Revelations* and is the patron saint of soldiers. Common from the twelfth century, since which time many spelling forms have been used. The name is internationally popular and has been a favourite during the present century.

Miriam (g) The earliest form of Mary and the name of Moses' sister who hid him in the bulrushes. From the Hebrew meaning Longed For Child it was adopted by the Puritans, and has always been popular with Jewish people.

Moira, Moyra (g) The English form of Maire, which is the Irish form of Mary. Like Maureen, also evolved from the Irish name Mairin, a diminutive of Maire, Moira has lost its entirely Irish associations and has become widely accepted as an independent name.

Molly (g) Long used as an independent name it was originally a pet form of Mary.

N

Naomi (g) A biblical name which in Hebrew means Pleasant. The name of the mother-in-law of Ruth in the famous story about Ruth and Naomi. The name was favoured by the Puritans in the seventeenth century, is popular with Jewish people and also in general use.

Natalia, Natalie (g) From the Latin words 'natale domini' meaning Birthday of the Lord. Natalie, the French version, is popular in English speaking countries. Natalia, less common, is the Russian form, whose diminutive Natasha is perhaps better known.

Natasha (g) Diminutive of Natalie now used as an independent name.

Nathan (b) Name of an Old Testament prophet it is Hebrew meaning Gift. Like many biblical names it was taken up by the Puritans. Although the name has always been more popular in America it has had a revival here in the last 20 years.

Nicola, Nicole, Nicolette (g) Nicola is the Italian and Nicole the French feminine forms of Nicholas, both of which have been influenced by the success of Nicholas during this century. Nicolette is a diminutive of Nicole from which Collette is derived.

Nigel, Neal, Neil, Naill (b) The various forms of Neal are believed to be derived from the Irish 'niadh' meaning Champion. There is also an Icelandic hero's name Njal. The name was introduced to Britain by the Normans as Nel, Neel, and Nele. This was Latinized to Nigellus, thought to be a diminutive of 'niger' meaning Black, from which Nigel evolved. Niall is generally used in Ireland, and Neil and Nigel in Scotland. They rose in popularity during the 1960s and have become widespread in all English-speaking countries.

O

Oliver (b) The origins are uncertain though the modern use is derived from the French for Olive Tree. In Latin it means Crowned with Olives. It is possible that the name is derived from an older source and has the same root as Olaf, also connected to the Old German Alav, meaning Relic and Ancestors. The name was fairly popular up to the seventeenth century, when Oliver Cromwell led the parliamentary revolution. The name fell from favour and was not revived until the nineteenth century.

Oscar (b) Old English meaning Godspear. The name was in use before the Conquest but seems to have died out until it was revived by James Macpherson whose Ossianic poems were published in the eighteenth century. The poems were supposed to be translations of works by the third-century bard, Ossian, who had a son called Oscar. They became all the rage and the name was given to Napoleon's grandson, who later became King of Sweden, popularizing and spreading the name throughout Europe.

Oswald (b) Old English meaning God Power. Oswestry took its name from St Oswald, who was King of Northumbria and died fighting the Welsh there in the seventh century. The name was favoured in the Middle Ages and has survived to the present, though its use is more limited now.

Owen (b) From the Welsh meaning Young Warrior or the Erse (Irish Gaelic) name Eoghan. There were many Eoghans in Ireland, one of them a King of Connaught. Probably the most influential Owen was Owen Glendower who fought for Welsh independence in the fifteenth century. The name has spread across Britain and over to America where it has come into general use especially with Welsh families.

P

Pamela (g) There are two sources for this name, Old German meaning Gift of the Elf, Sagacity and Inborn Intellect, or Greek meaning All Honey. Its use in Britain seems to date from the sixteenth-century romance *Arcadia* written by Sir Philip Sidney. The name was only taken up generally after the publication of Samuel Richardson's novel, *Pamela* in 1740.

Patience (g) Another of the abstract virtue names popular with the Puritans in the seventeenth century. It is one of the few that have remained in use, unlike some of the more extreme examples which fell from favour after the Restoration.

Patricia (g) The feminine form of Patrick which dates back to the eighteenth century. Its use this century was influenced by Princess Patricia of Connaught, granddaughter of Queen Victoria. Most popular during the 1950s and still very much in general use today.

Patrick (b) Latin meaning Nobleman. St Patrick the fifth-century saint was born in Scotland but captured by pirates and sold as a slave in Ireland. He escaped and trained as a missionary in France only to return to devote his life to converting the Irish to Christianity. In Scotland the name was interchangeable with Peter, and common during the Middle Ages when it spread to England. The name is in general use in Britain but most popular in Ireland and with families of Irish descent.

Paul (b) Latin meaning Small and the name taken by St Paul the Apostle on his conversion to Christianity; previously he was called Saul of Tarsus. Paul has often been connected with Peter and the two saints share the same feast day. The name has been in general use since the seventeenth century but it is only during this century that it has gained favour.

Paula, Pauline (g) Also from the Latin for Small. St Paula founded several convents in Bethlehem in the fourth century and, because of her, the name was a popular choice in the Middle Ages. Pauline is the French form and often used as feminine of Paul. Pauline was a Roman girls' name, though it is rarely used today.

Penelope (g) The first part of the name is connected with the Greek word meaning Bobbin. It is also possibly Celtic, from the Irish Finnghuala, meaning White Shouldered. In Homer's Odyssey, Penelope waited ten years for her husband Odysseus to return from the Trojan War. She turned down many offers to remarry, saying she had to finish her weaving first. There was little chance of that, as she kept unravelling it in the hope that her husband would return. The name has always been more popular in Ireland where it is sometimes interchanged with Fenella and Ursula.

Phillipa (g) The Latin feminine of Philip and the name of Chaucer's wife. It has been used steadily during the last couple of centuries but is not common. Pippa and Phil are the usual pet forms.

Polly (g) An English pet form of Mary. It possibly evolved because it rhymes with Molly, another pet form of Mary. Polly is also a pet name for Pauline. Popularized by its use in nursery rhymes such as 'Polly Put The Kettle On', and 'Little Polly Flinders', it has been used as an independent name and is also sometimes coupled with Anna to make Pollyanna or Pollyann.

Priscilla (g) Derived from the Roman name Prisca, meaning Ancient. She was the wife of the Roman Jew Aquila, and mentioned in the Acts of the Apostles. Another New Testament name taken up by the Puritans which has remained in limited use.

Prunella (g) Its history is obscure though it is believed to come from the French for Plum Coloured. A familiar but uncommon name.

R

Randal, Randolph (b) Derived from the Old English 'Randwulf' meaning Shield or House Wolf. The Normans brought their own version of the name to England and the forms Ranulf, Randal and Randle became popular during the Middle Ages. Randolph was derived from the Latinized form Randulfus during the eighteenth century. Randal and Randolph are the forms in modern use. Randy is a shortened version which is sometimes used as an independent name in America.

Rex (b) Latin meaning King. It is also a short form for Reginald but seems to have become divorced from that association and is increasingly used as an independent name.

Rhona (g) Possibly derived from the Welsh name Rhonwen see Rowena.

Rita (g) Originally a short form for the French version of Margaret, Marguerite and the Italian version, Margherita. It is also used as an independent name and was made popular earlier this century by the American film star Rita Hayworth.

Roderick (b) Old German meaning Famous ruler. The name is a favourite in Scotland where in early times it was confused with the Gaelic name Ruaridh, meaning Red, until Roderick became the accepted version. The name is well known in most English speaking countries with Rod, Roddy and Roddie as the usual short forms.

Rodney (b) Originally a placename in Somerset meaning Reed Island which was adopted as a surname. In the eighteenth century Admiral George Rodney popularized the name and it was taken up as a Christian name around this time. It shares the same short forms as Roderick.

Roger (b) Anglo-Saxon from Hrothgar meaning Fame Spear. There is also an Old German source which came over with the Normans meaning Spearman. It was widely used as a peasant name during the sixteenth and seventeenth centuries. An ancient variation, Hodge, was associated with farm labourers and, by the eighteenth century, some people considered it too countrified to be fashionable. It was still used as a traditional family name, however, and by the nineteenth century had regained much of its earlier popularity. It is still in widespread use today.

Ronald, Ranald (b) Originally Scottish equivalents of Reginald and Reynold, Ronald has been absorbed into general use. Unlike Ranald, it has lost its exclusively Scottish associations.

Rory, Rorie (b) Celtic meaning Red. Popular in Ireland due to the influence of the twelfth-century king Rory O'Connor and two other Irish monarchs. The name is also popular in Scotland, especially in the Highlands, and is sometimes used as a short form for Roderick.

Rosalie (g) This is the French form of the Latin Rosalia, and also the name of a Roman festival when tombs were draped with roses. The twelfth-century saint Rosalia, patron saint of Palermo, is believed to have initiated its use as a Christian name.

Rosalind (g) Always very popular because of its literary associations, Rosalind was the heroine of Shakespeare's *As You Like It*. The name came to England from Spain during the reign of Elizabeth I. The Goths took it to Spain and its original meaning was Horse Serpent. In Spanish, however, rosa means Rose and linda means Pretty – thus it was as Pretty Rose that the name arrived in England.

Rosamund (g) Another name of Old German origin meaning Horse Protection which, when translated from the Latin rosa munda, means Pure Rose, or from rosa mundi, Rose of the World. The Latin roots became the accepted versions and the name has remained with us down the centuries. Rosamond, the French version, is also in widespread use.

Rose (g) This simple version, including its alternative Rosie, is the best loved flower name of all. There is an Old German form from Hros, meaning Horse. However, in England the name has always been associated with the flower. The Normans introduced the name as Roese and Rohese but its simplest form, Rose, has withstood the test of time. Along with Rosa it was at its most popular at the turn of the century, but has continued in use, both on its own and as part of many compound names.

Roslyn, Rosalyn (g) Rosslyn, Roslynn and Roslin are alternative forms. The name is a compound of Rose and Lyn, a variant of Rosalind and a Scottish place-name.

Roy (b) There are Gaelic and Celtic sources both meaning Red, or it could come from the French *roi* for King. The name was perpetuated in Scotland by the Famous red-haired Rob Roy (Robert Macgregor), who was involved in the Rising of 1715, and later by Sir Walter Scott's celebrated novel *Rob Roy*. Although the name has never lost its Scottish links it has become very widespread in general use.

Rupert (b) From the same root as Robert and meaning Fame Bright. Prince Rupert of the Rhine was King Charles I's nephew and a gallant and dashing supporter of the Royalist cause. This romantic hero, along with the poet Rupert Brooke, whose tragic and untimely death during World War I endeared him to the British people, perpetuated and distinguished the name, although its use is now limited.

Ryan (b) Probably from the Gaelic. An Irish surname which has been adopted as a Christian name and taken into general use. Recently Ryan has become popular in both England and America.

S

Sally (g) A pet form of Sarah which has been in use since the seventeenth century.

Samantha (g) Possibly derived from an Aramaic word meaning Listener. The name was rarely used before this century but is now extremely popular. Sam and Sammy are the usual pet forms.

Sandra (g) Originally a short version of the Italian name, Alessandra, which since the middle of this century has been used as a name in its own right. It is also short for the English Alexandra.

Sara, Sarah (g) Hebrew meaning Princess, Sara is the Greek form and Zara the Eastern. After the Reformation, Sarah and its diminutives Sally, Sairey and Sadie became very popular in England. Sarah and the alternative Sara are still a favourite choice today. Sarotte is the French form, and the Celtic names Sorcha meaning Bright and Saraid, meaning Excellent, are Irish equivalent names.

Sean (b) Generally recognized as the Irish for John. From the Old French Jehan which, in modern form, is Jean. The name is very widespread although it has not entirely lost its Irish associations and is used by families with Irish connections. Alternatives include Shaun and Shane which is an American variation.

Sharon (g) Hebrew meaning The Plain. A biblical placename which was used by the Puritans who took it to America with them. The name was revived to become a favourite choice around the middle of this century in most English speaking countries, though it seems to have peaked and is less popular today.

Sheila (g) From the Irish Sile, itself a form of Celia or Cecilia, which was taken to Ireland in Norman times. Sheila is the English spelling which is very common in English speaking countries and which seems to have lost its exclusively Irish origins. Sheela, Sheelah and Sheelagh are Irish variant spellings which are also spreading into general use.

Sidney, Sydney (m) Originally a surname which was probably adopted from St Denis, the French town, and brought to England by the Sydney family who settled here during the reign of Henry II. Sir Philip Sidney, the Elizabethan poet and soldier and later Algernon Sidney, the seventeenth-century Republican, popularized the name. Like many distinguished surnames, it was adopted for use as a personal name by the general public. Viscount Sydney, who was Secretary of State during the nineteenth century, gave his name to the city in Australia.

Sonia, Sonya (g) The Russian pet form of Sophia which was adopted here during this century.

Sophia, Sophie (g) Greek meaning The Wisdom of God. A niece of Justinian was named Sophia after the great cathedral Hagia Sophia at Constantinople, which he claimed surpassed Solomon's. The name was popular in the Eastern church and spread to Hungary, Germany and hence to England with George I, whose wife and mother were both named Sophia.

Stephanie (g) The French feminine form of Stephen, now so popular in English speaking countries that its French connections have almost been forgotten.

Stuart, Stewart (b) The name of the Royal House of Scotland which was founded by Walter the High Steward, and which gave us four kings and two queens. From Old English Sti Weard, an official, or steward in charge of the animals kept for food. Because of the romanticism of the Stuart cause in the eighteenth century the name was adopted as a Christian name and especially favoured in the nineteenth century. Although it has never entirely lost its Scottish associations, the name retains its popularity to the present day.

T

Tamsin (g) Tamsin is the most well known although Tamara and Tamasine are also variant forms of Thomasina, the feminine form of Thomas. Tammy, the pet form, is also used as an individual name.

Tania, Tanya (g) Pet forms of the popular Russian name Tatiana, the name of a third-century martyr of the Russian Orthodox church. Now recognized in English speaking countries as an independent name.

Tara (g) A new name taken from an old name marking the coronation site of the Irish kings. In the book and the film *Gone With The Wind* it was the name of the plantation left to Scarlett O'Hara. The massive success of the movie familiarized Tara, which has recently become a popular name in America and Canada.

Timothy (b) Greek from Timotheos meaning To Honour God and also connected with the Latin Timor, meaning fear. Timothy was companion to St Paul and his name was taken up in Europe during the sixteenth century when the Bible was a popular source of Christian names. Timothea is a rare feminine form.

Tina (g) A short form for Christina and other names ending in -tina which is now recognized as an independent name.

Tobias, Toby (b) Hebrew meaning God is Good, although there is another interpretation meaning A Poet. The story of 'Tobias and the Angel' from the Apocrypha was a favourite in the Middle Ages and Toby the Punch and Judy dog is named after the dog which accompanied Tobias on his travels in the story. Tobias is the Greek form, and Toby is the English which was common in the seventeenth and eighteenth centuries when the Toby Jug was dedicated to the famous drinker, Toby Philpot.

U

Ursula (g) Latin meaning Little She-bear. St Ursula was a fifth-century Cornish Princess shipwrecked near Cologne and murdered along with her companions. A teaching order of nuns was founded in her name. Ursula was featured in Shakespeare's *Much Ado About Nothing* and in the celebrated nineteenth-century novel *John Halifax, Gentleman* by Mrs Craik, which did much to revive public interest in the name. Usella is an alternative spelling that is rarely used.

V

Valerie (g) From the Roman family name Valeria, which comes from the verb To be in Good Health. Valerie was the French version, adopted in Britain in the late nineteenth century, and still in regular use today.

Vanessa (g) Vanessa Redgrave is probably the best known example of this name which was created by Jonathan Swift, the poet, in the eighteenth century as a pet name for Ester Vanhomrigh.

Vera (g) Slavonic meaning Grace of Love and Faith; also Russian meaning Faith, or alternatively Latin for True. The name came into fashion at the turn of the century when there was a vogue for Russian names. Although popular in the 1920s, the name has since fallen from favour with modern parents.

Victor (b) The name was introduced in England as the male form of Victoria during the reign of Queen Victoria. From the Latin meaning Victor.

Victoria (g) Latin meaning Victory. The name was uncommon until the reign of Queen Victoria who was named after her mother. Strangely enough, it was not a particularly popular name until the recent resurgence of Victorian nostalgia. Vicky or Vickie is the usual short form.

Vivian (b) From the Latin meaning Lively. Although the name dates back to the twelfth century in Britain it has never been common. A contemporary example is Sir Vivien Fuchs, the famous Antarctic explorer.

Vivien (g) The feminine of Vivian taken from the French form Vivienne. Tennyson perpetuated the name in his poem 'Vivien and Merlin'. Vivien Leigh, star of the epic film, *Gone With The Wind* is a more modern example.

W

Walter (b) An Old German name meaning Daring Ruler and popular with the Normans who established it in Britain after the Conquest. Sir Walter Raleigh and Sir Walter Scott must have contributed to the popularity of the name over the centuries. Wat is the older short form, while Wally or Walt are the modern diminutives.

Warren (b) From an Old German folk name meaning Protector, Defending Warrior. Introduced by the Normans as Warin and Guarin, from which the surnames Warren, Waring and Garnet evolved. Its use as a Christian name almost died out but was revived during the nineteenth century. It is more widespread in America than Britain.

Wayne (b) Old English from 'wain' meaning Wagon. A surname which was first adopted as a Christian name in America and has now become very popular in Britain. Celebrated holders include British dancer and choreographer, Wayne Sleep.

Wendy (g) The name was created by Margaret Henley, a child friend of author James Barrie whom she called 'Friendy-Wendy'. He used it in his celebrated children's classic *Peter Pan and Wendy* and the name has been a favourite ever since.

X

Xenia (g) Greek meaning Host. Zenia is an alternative form, though both names are uncommon.

Z

Zachariah, Zacharias, Zachary (b) Hebrew meaning Remembrance or God Has Remembered. Zacharias is the Greek form and Zachary the English form which occurred in the Middle Ages to be revived by Puritans who exported it to America where it is still in use. Zach and Zak are the usual short forms.

Zita (g) A modern development of names ending in -ita or -sita, which is particularly liked in Australia.

Zoe (g) Greek meaning Life. In the third century the Alexandrian Jews equated it with Eve as 'the mother of life'. The name spread throughout the Eastern Church but has only been used in England since the nineteenth century. It is now becoming increasingly popular both in Britain and America.

THE FAMILY MATTERS SERIES